BIGGER

BIGGER

REBUILDING THE BROKEN

KRISTAN DOOLEY

NEW YORK

Bigger
Rebuilding the Broken

Published in New York, New York, by Morgan James Publishing. Morgan James and The Entrepreneurial Publisher are trademarks of Morgan James, LLC.

The Morgan James Speakers Group can bring authors to your live event. For more information or to book an event visit The Morgan James Speakers Group at: www.TheMorganJamesSpeakersGroup.com.

Morgan James Publishing
The Entrepreneurial Publisher
Office (212) 655-5470
www.MorganJamesPublishing.com

bitlit

A **free** eBook edition is available with the purchase of this print book.

CLEARLY PRINT YOUR NAME ABOVE IN UPPER CASE

Instructions to claim your free eBook edition:
1. Download the BitLit app for Android or iOS
2. Write your name in **UPPER CASE** on the line
3. Use the BitLit app to submit a photo
4. Download your eBook to any device

First Edition

9781630476212   paperback
9781630476229   eBook

Library of Congress Control Number: 2015905275

Cover Design by:
CrossBooks
A Division of LifeWay

Interior Design by:
Brittany Bondar
www.Sage-Words.com

In an effort to support local communities, raise awareness and funds, Morgan James Publishing donates a percentage of all book sales for the life of each book to Habitat for Humanity Peninsula and Greater Williamsburg.

Get involved today, visit
www.MorganJamesBuilds.com

To my husband:
Thank you for believing in me and never doubting God's call,
for chasing after the *bigger* and never settling for less.

To my girls:
You have taught me so much about God's relentless love.
If He loves me even half as much as I love you,
then we're all good.

To Yosselin:
How great were His plans! What an honor to journey toward
bigger with you. Thank you for allowing us the privilege.
Brokenness always leads to *bigger*, when placed in the
hands of the Master Rebuilder.

TABLE OF CONTENTS

SECTION FOUR

LIVING OUT BIGGER

FOREWORD

We live in a fragmented, fragile world. Sometimes we can find ourselves ambushed by hope and often from places and people right in our own neighborhoods and communities. For all of the pain, fear, and uncertainty in the world there is an undercurrent of humanity, generosity, and brotherly love that flows through us all.

I've known this for quite some time, but I saw it come to life in Yosselin's story. In 2012, my younger son was a sixth grader at Cherokee Elementary School in Liberty Township, Ohio. He came home from school one day with the sort of news you hope you never have to hear from a kid. One of his schoolmates, Yosselin, had been diagnosed with cancer. My heart went out to her and her family, but, shamefully, I took no immediate action. I didn't know the family personally. It seemed best (read: *easier*) to pray for them and hope for the best from a distance.

Luckily, I have friends more willing to take action. Two couples from my church heard of Yosselin's diagnosis. They discovered that Yosselin's family needed help. One of them, Kristan Dooley, was my friend and workmate. I watched as she and her husband, Dave, courageously led a group of people to provide Yosselin and her family with the perfect house for this brave little girl to live in while she beat cancer.

I thank God that I was able to witness a grassroots movement of people who sacrificed their time, talent, and money to let one little girl know that she is loved by us and by God. I played a very small part in this story, but it was enough for me to know that this is what life is all about—a community of people expressing genuine love and expecting nothing in return.

I'm thrilled that Kristan has written this book. This is a story that reminds us that the greatest miracles are possible when normal people come together in the spirit of generosity. This story will make you laugh, cry, and believe in something bigger than us. Just be careful . . . it may also make you the sort of person who will take bold action while others sit idly by.

Joe Boyd
Founder and President, Rebel Pilgrim Productions

INTRODUCTION

In January, God handed me the word *bigger*. Sitting in the back of staff prayer, tears running down my cheeks, I tried to hand it back to Him. *Bigger* didn't make sense. Just the day before my family met Yosselin. Pulling out of Yosselin's driveway that cold afternoon my heart broke into a million pieces.

Yosselin sat next to Ella, my first grader at Wyandot Elementary. The two girls had quickly become good friends. For the past two weeks Yosselin hadn't been to school and her new friend, Ella, was more than concerned. Our quest to find out why led us to the discovery of more than we intended. Yosselin had cancer.

A few days later, my family piled into the car and headed to Yosselin's house. We didn't know them, but we knew we had to go. During the short drive, I gave Ella an introduction to what it means to have cancer. Yosselin had already started chemo and I feared the side effects might be confusing or frightening for Ella, making it difficult for her to be the friend Yosselin needed right now.

Looking through my rearview mirror I choked back tears as I watched Ella put her brave face on. Tears welled up in her big blue eyes as she struggled to fully understand what was happening to her friend. As we turned our car onto their gravel driveway, we each took a deep breath and pulled ourselves together.

The Randalls welcomed us into their home, their lives, and their brokenness. Pulling back out of their driveway that afternoon, I knew things would never be the same. It wasn't by accident Ella sat next to Yosselin. It wasn't by accident we met this family. I knew there was more but, unable to see the bigger picture, all I could see was I couldn't fix what was broken.

After a long night and little sleep I found myself the next morning at staff prayer. Unable to listen to anything going on up front, I sat in the back of the chapel and cried. I threw all my questions before God. Why Yosselin? Why Ella? Why this family? What was our connection? What did He want us to do? What was He going to do? Coming to the end of myself I whispered, *"Give me something to go on, God. I am having a hard time understanding where You are in all of this. Just give me a word, say something, anything, so I know You are here."*

As I cried and prayed I felt the Spirit of God whisper back to me, *"bigger."* *"Bigger,"* that was it, not healing, not hope, not love, not trust—just *"bigger."* I wrestled with Him for a few minutes, desperately searching my heart for other words. Words I thought would better fit the situation at hand. But over and over again I found myself back at *"bigger."*

God speaks to us on a daily basis. It's what we do with what we hear that makes the difference. Learning to recognize the voice of God is an art. Hearing is a muscle that can be developed and toned. Increasing our ability to recognize and respond to His voice takes practice, patience, and persistence.

The other day I thought He asked me to pray for this woman bagging my groceries at Kroger. Knots quickly formed in my stomach as I began to offer up to Him every excuse possible. Trying to find the courage to say the first word, I made eye contact with her as she handed me my groceries. I opened my mouth, but nothing came out. She quickly looked away, leaving me feeling rejected and disappointed. I muttered, "Thank you," then bolted to my car.

I argued with myself as I drove home from the store. Just that morning I had prayed and asked God to help me see people the way He saw them. I desired to be a conduit of His blessing. To be bold with what I saw and felt. I wanted to trust God more than my own need for acceptance or understanding. I definitely didn't imagine running to my car to hide.

Good thing we serve a God more concerned with our hearts than with our ability to get it right every time. "Does the Lord delight in burnt offerings and sacrifices as much as in obeying the Lord? To obey is better than sacrifice" (1 Sam. 15:22). God's biggest desire is for us to have hearts longing to recognize and respond to His voice.

God is a God of infinite grace because we *are* going to get it wrong. This life is a journey and as we travel we are going to struggle. In the midst of those struggles, we will fail. Thankfully, He doesn't focus on our failures as much as He focuses on our hearts. He hasn't placed the responsibility of bringing His kingdom to earth fully on our shoulders. Rather, He has invited us to partner with Him as He ushers in that which we cannot.

God wants a relationship, one that goes deep. He wants to tell us things, show us things, and move us in His direction. He delights in us as we learn to better recognize and respond to His voice—even when we get it wrong. Even when we misunderstand, He is richly satisfied with us. His grace compels us to keep trying. Knowing it is not about us and what we can or cannot do frees us to step into *bigger*. *Bigger* is all about Him and what He has already done.

The desire of my heart is to be obedient. I want to hear what God says. My Father recognizes the desire of my heart and that is enough. I believe my two girls, Ella and Addilyn, want to be obedient. I don't think they spend their days plotting how to rebel against the rules of our home. Sure, they may sometimes bump up against an expectation here or there, but in most cases, their little hearts are pure. They desire to please Mom and Dad. They desire to respond appropriately and for that I am extremely happy. Are they going to get it right every time? No way! They mess up, they misunderstand, and they even misrepresent our family at times.

When the girls make mistakes, my husband, Dave, and I don't stop talking to them. We don't shun them or excommunicate them from the family. Instead we use their mistakes to teach them. On the other side of our misunderstandings are opportunities for growth. There will always be consequences for their wrong actions, but our hope is for increased maturity on the other side of those consequences.

As our Father, Abba God does the same with us. He digs deep and focuses in on the desire of our hearts. He recognizes the difference between a heart driven by relationship and intimacy with Him and a heart driven by religion and rules. It is in the place of relationship that we learn how to hear and respond to the voice of God. It is in this place we are free to step out, mess up, and, at the same time, still embrace more of Him. Here we are free to wrestle with the struggle of obedience and surrender.

This word, *bigger*, started me on a journey. As I have journeyed toward *bigger* with Him by my side, my mind has been radically transformed. I was at the end of my rope, completely out of ideas, unable to fix what was broken, when God stepped in. He stepped in and whispered, *"bigger,"* to my desperate heart that cold morning in January. This time I refused to allow doubt to squash what I believed He said. I refused to pass up the opportunity to see what He meant for fear of getting it wrong. I decided to take Him at His word. I took what I felt, even though it didn't make sense, and I gave it back to God with anticipation.

If He gave me this word, then it was because He intended to do something with it. Something I couldn't do without Him. God gives revelation; it is what we do with revelation that makes the difference. I simply gave what I was sensing back to the only One capable of making something out of it. Quietly I prayed, *"Father, I'm not sure what you mean. I feel so helpless. This family, this diagnosis, this situation. It's all too big. I'm not sure I can do anything to help, but if 'bigger' is the word, then please be bigger now. I need you to be bigger. They need you to be bigger. We all need you to be bigger."* I said amen, closed my prayer journal, wiped the tears from my eyes, and waited.

It didn't take long to realize *bigger* wasn't just for Yosselin. *Bigger* was for me. *Bigger* was for my faith and my ability to believe God is exactly who He says He is. *Bigger* was for my future, and for my capacity to trust Him in ways I never thought I would. It was for my family and for the way He intended to rebuild us. *Bigger* was for my friends. Believing *bigger* changed my perception, helping me better discern the heart of the Father. Believing *bigger* transformed my mind and allowed me to step more confidently into the person He created me to be.

Since this season, God has had me on a journey toward *bigger*. Over and over again as we spend time together He invites me to recognize brokenness in my life and challenged me to trust Him with it. It hasn't been easy. In fact, I would say I have surrendered more than any other year's prior. I would say I have cried more tears, dealt with more anger and raw emotions than ever before. I have struggled to understand and overcome the fear of the unknown, but I haven't quit. My desire to hear and respond to His voice compels me to keep going. The promise of *bigger* motivates me to try again tomorrow.

It amazes me how something can be so challenging and costly, yet also extremely rewarding at the same time. I am thankful we serve a God who is *bigger* than the brokenness threatening to overtake us. I am thankful He finds us in our brokenness, picks up our heavy load, and walks us through the process of transformation aligning us to His *bigger* purposes.

God had *bigger* in store for Yosselin and her family. He didn't intend to leave them in a broken-down home with a broken diagnosis and a less than appealing future. He intended to move them toward *bigger*.

God had more in store for me. He never intended to leave me there rebuilding the brokenness of my family and friends. He intended to help me open my hands back and surrender to His *bigger* plan and His rebuilding process.

This book is simply an invitation to journey with me. No matter where you are, God has more in store for you. He wants to increase your ability to trust and depend on Him. He wants to restore what's been broken in your life and in the lives of those around you. If you call out to Him, He promises to answer. What we do with what He tells us makes all the difference in the world.

section one

BIGGER THINGS

chapter one

The Start of Something

YOSSELIN'S STORY

We met Yosselin in January. Yosselin was the reason I thought I needed the word *bigger*. She sat next to my daughter, Ella, in their first grade classroom, which is a miracle in and of itself because I never intended to put Ella in school. I spent the entire summer wrestling with God over the school issue. I assumed my surrender was coming in the form of doing whatever it took to educate my children outside of the public school system, but the lack of peace inside left me wondering what God was trying to say.

Turns out surrender came in the shape of Wyandot Elementary School, where Ella would start first grade that year. Ella and Yosselin became quick friends. In November Yosselin was diagnosed with osteosarcoma, a rapidly growing form of bone cancer. She had a tumor in her right femur and numerous nodes in both lungs. When the cancer forced her out of school and into chemo, Ella noticed.

Every day, she came home, "Mom, Yosselin wasn't in school today. Mom, Yosselin was sick again. Mom, do you think she is on vacation? Mom, do you think she is okay? Mom, will you call Ms. O'Keefe and see if Yosselin is alright?" On and on she went, every day, relentlessly. Something wasn't right and Ella sensed it.

I sensed it too, which was part of the reason I didn't want to ask. Knowledge brought responsibility and that scared me.

But eventually Ella's persistence wore me down. I e-mailed Marilyn, the girls' teacher: *Hi, Marilyn, Ella has come home every day for a few weeks now concerned about Yosselin and her absence. I know you might not be able to talk about what's going on but with Dave*

and I being pastors at the Vineyard, we would love to know if
there is anything we could do to help this family.

The next morning, as I rounded the corner to walk Ella to class,
Marilyn was waiting for me by the lockers. I could tell by the
look on her face things were not okay. My heart sank deep into
my stomach. Every part of me wanted to turn around and not
hear whatever it was she was about to tell me. She pulled me
aside and let me in on what was going on with Yosselin. Yosselin
had cancer. The cancer had spread so rapidly that doctors
immediately pulled her out of school and put her in chemo.
Her future was unknown at this point. All that was known was
that her family was in for the fight of their lives.

A few weeks later, we picked Ella up from school and headed
over to meet Yosselin and her family for the first time. Little did
we know the *bigger* things God had in store for our families.
Pulling into their driveway, we met Yosselin's grandma and
grandpa, Keith and Tammy Randall. Keith and Tammy had full
custody of Yosselin and her little brother, Freddy. Not surpris-
ingly, the news of Yosselin's cancer brought reality crashing
down in their world. They were nearing the end of their strength
and needed more of God, not just in a physical, healing way,
but also in a spiritual, relational way. They needed *bigger*.

As if the news of Yosselin's cancer weren't bad enough for this
devastated family, the house they were living in seemed to be
falling down around them. Over the past two years the family's
house had been severely damaged by floodwaters. The force of
the water under the floorboards of the house literally shifted
the foundation, leaving this family in extremely hazardous living conditions. They were in the middle of repairing the flood
damage when the cancer was discovered.

Yosselin, now on a walker because of the tumor in her right leg, had been moved downstairs into the unfinished front room of the house. Her new room broke my heart. The room was less than ideal for a little girl battling off infection. A makeshift floor allowed Yosselin to walk through the room on the walker. The open chimney and windows were covered in plastic in an attempt to keep out the drafty January air and in the corner sat a portable toilet because Yosselin could no longer make it through the crooked bathroom door on her walker. My eyes were drawn to the little pink get-well balloon that hung on the powdery, unfinished drywall over her bed and as I stared at it, my heart shattered into a million pieces.

In a matter of weeks, this little girl had been stripped of so much. It was hard to breathe as I imagined my own daughter facing what Yosselin was facing. I choked back tears and tried my hardest to be strong, but picturing Yosselin in this room for the next year, fighting off infection and circumstances she didn't ask for, made it hard to swallow.

What do you do when your child has cancer? How do you maneuver in such an intense reality? The level of brokenness going on in the life of this family overwhelmed me. As we sat at their kitchen table that cold, dreary afternoon and listened to them describe the past few weeks, my own problems seemed to slip away.

It's a natural response to want to fix broken things. No one wants to look into the eyes of a hurting, broken person and have nothing to offer them. But there would be no quick fix for Yosselin's situation. Unable to fix this families' broken-ness quickly brought me to the end of myself. I would soon discover that at the end of myself was exactly where God wanted me to be.

"Can I share your story with my friends?" I asked Tammy before we left. "I can't make any promises, I don't know what we can do, but I know people who pray and I would love to share this with them." Through her tears she hugged me and told me the more people praying, the better.

Backing out of their driveway I turned to Dave, "Okay, what do we do? How do we fix this?"

Dave looked at me with huge tears in his eyes, shook his head, and murmured the words I feared most, "We can't fix this. They need a new house. This house needs to be torn down and a new one put in its place."

I don't think we spoke the rest of the night. We drove home in silence, we ate dinner in silence, and we went to bed in silence. We were both too overcome with grief to pretend everything was normal. I could not undo what I had just seen. I could not push away what I was feeling. God broke my heart for this family. It was in pieces, completely nonfunctional, useless pieces.

The next morning was when God gave me the word *bigger*. That's why upon first hearing the Spirit whisper *"bigger"* over my heart I assumed the word was for Yosselin. I needed a word for what this family was facing. I needed something to help process all we had encountered, something to make sense of it.

I thought *bigger* was for Yosselin, her family, and their situation. I was right, but the truth is, *bigger* was for so much more. I love how God is so massive and so good at what He does that He will allow the brokenness in the lives of others to show us the brokenness in our own lives. I had no idea of the journey I was about to begin. I had no clue how my prayers for more of God on behalf of Yosselin and her family would shape the next year of my life. I never would have guessed how *bigger* would be what God used to do a transforming work in my life.

I thought it was for Yosselin. I thought it was for the Randall family, for the cancer, for the broken-down house and for everyone that would watch as God showed up again and again to do what only He could do. Man, was I wrong.

Surrendering to *bigger* moved my family into a place of action. Now we were able to see how little we could do on our own. We needed God to do something we couldn't. Nothing was impossible with Him, but everything was impossible without Him. Embracing *bigger* on behalf of Yosselin and her family meant stepping into the impossible and expecting God to show up.

SMALL BEGINNINGS

While we waited for God to do what only He could do, we started doing the things we knew how to do. We knew how to buy gas cards, provide meals, and show the Randalls they were not walking this road alone. My dad and Dave put together a plan to rehab the front room Yosselin was living in. If she was going to be stuck inside the house between chemo rounds, we wanted her room to be the happiest place it could be. With each step, every donated meal, and every picture someone hung on the wall, I pushed myself to remember what God had told us and I prayed for *bigger*.

When we are faced with circumstances out of our control, God's heart is to do more than we ever asked or imagine possible, but God had to first get us to the place where we would be willing to believe the impossible. God delights in small beginnings because those first steps are always important faith builders. With each step He showed up and each time He showed up miracles took place. With each miracle our faith increased and our ability to believe in more grew.

One evening while we were painting the walls of Yosselin's beautiful new room, Dave pulled me out of the crowded space with a concerned look on his face. "Do you realize we have all these people here painting these walls and God is going to tear this house down and build a new one?"

Absolutely, I knew that. I had already begun to recognize the dream God was birthing in our hearts. I was realizing the *bigger*. *Bigger* wasn't fixing this broken house, *bigger* was tearing it down and building a new one. I recognized what God was doing in me. He was increasing my faith so I would trust Him to do the impossible in the future. My prayer was that He was also doing the same in my friends as they worked. Small beginnings are necessary steps.

We don't jump from the broken to the *bigger*; it's a process, a one step at a time journey.

Over the course of the next ten months we rallied together and followed God as He led us toward *bigger* on behalf of Yosselin and her family. Healing was essential. A new house was crucial. This family recognizing how big God is and how much He loved them was necessary. We worked hard, but God worked harder. Piece by piece the project came together. God opened door after door in order to ensure we continued progressing toward *bigger*. There aren't enough pages in this book to tell you all of the amazing things He did as we continued the journey.

In June, we moved Yosselin and her family into temporary housing so their existing house could be torn down and construction on the new house could begin. It came together exactly as needed, until one evening we were standing together in a brand new, $300,000, handicap-accessible, fully donated, completely furnished, breathtakingly beautiful house.

The night of the house reveal I looked in awe and amazement. This is what He meant by *bigger*. He meant these people, this team, the past ten exhausting months, the impossible dream. He meant the Randalls, who trusted a complete stranger's belief in God's goodness. He meant the neighbors crowded around outside the house with welcome home signs and cameras. He meant the local news stations, who caught wind of the story and wanted to share it with the world.

This was *bigger*. *Bigger* than I'd ever imagined possible. It was hard to believe eight months earlier I struggled to breathe as we prayed with this family we had just met and now here we were on the other side of brokenness, made breathless yet again, only this time not by the destruction surrounding us, but by the faithfulness of God. I am still in complete awe of all God accomplished as we followed Him through the *bigger* process of rebuilding.

BIGGER STILL

The crazy part is, the entire time God was working *through* me to move Yosselin's family toward *bigger*, He was also working in me to move me toward *bigger*. He is so multifaceted like that. God was not only interested in rebuilding Yosselin's brokenness; He was interested in rebuilding my brokenness. Partnering with Him through this project changed me.

While walking with Yosselin God gave me a taste of all He is capable of. He opened my eyes to what living in step with His Spirit looks like. He exposed me to His heart and invited me into the unknown. I learned God is the only qualified rebuilder of what's broken. Only He can put lives back together in a way that makes perfect sense.

Before meeting Yosselin, my daily prayers included me asking God to show me who He really was. I was longing for intimacy with Him. I knew there had to be more. After Yosselin, God had not only shown me who He really is, but He had shown me who I really am. A transformation took place in the deepest part of me. He had changed me. He changed my relationship with Him.

Something was different between us. The connection we had was much stronger. I burn for Him. I ache to hear His voice every day, all the time. I long to follow Him wherever He wants to go, to see the world the way He sees the world. At the end of myself, I realized the most important thing I could do was connect to Him. I had found my most productive place, in His presence. I had made a life being busy for all kinds of good things, but somehow missed the best thing.

On the other side of brokenness, people are different. On the other side of brokenness, Yosselin was different. She knows Jesus differently. She may look like a normal little girl, but she isn't. She encountered the presence of God in her brokenness. He came down to her, picked her up, and pieced her back together. Not only did He heal her body—she is completely cancer free—but He also healed her soul!

On the other side of brokenness, Keith and Tammy are different. They live differently, they love differently, they trust differently. On the other side of brokenness, my community is different. We see ourselves differently, we see our kids differently, and we see God in our lives differently. On the other side of brokenness, I am different. I know God differently. We have been through the fire and He has proven Himself bigger.

THE PROMISED LAND

Moses was a faithful leader of the Israelite people for years. After his death, his protégé, Joshua, was left with big shoes to fill. As Joshua stood looking at the Jordan River, he must have been shaking in his sandals. Standing behind him, his people may have been confident in their new leader, but surely Joshua struggled to believe.

How in the world was he supposed to follow Moses as leader? Was he ready for the task at hand? Had he studied hard enough? Did he have the right connection with God? What if he failed? What if his people rejected him? Joshua's many fears and doubts left him ample ammunition to postpone stepping forward into the unknown. No one would have blamed him for choosing to stay this side of the Jordan, where life was smaller but predictable. Maybe he should just settle.

Then God spoke to Joshua,

> "Moses, my servant, is dead. Get ready! Cross the Jordan River! Lead these people into the land which I am ready to hand over to them. I am handing over to you every place you set foot, as I promised Moses. Your territory will

extend from the wilderness in the south to Lebanon in the north. It will extend all the way to the great River Euphrates in the east (including all of Syria) and all the way to the Mediterranean Sea in the west. No one will be able to resist you all the days of your life. As I was with Moses, so I will be with you. I will not abandon you or leave you alone. Be strong and brave! You must lead these people in the conquest of this land that I solemnly promised their ancestors I would hand over to them. Make sure you are very strong and brave! Carefully obey all the law my servant Moses charged you to keep. Do not swerve from it to the right or to the left, so that you may be successful in all you do. This law scroll must not leave your lips! You must memorize it day and night so you can carefully obey all that is written in it. Then you will prosper and be successful. I repeat, be strong and brave! Don't be afraid and don't panic, for I, the LORD your God, am with you in all you do." (Josh. 1:2–9 NET)

After receiving his charge, Joshua's doubts turn to anticipation. He turned from fear to face his people, "Go through the camp and command the people, 'Prepare your supplies, for within three days you will cross the Jordan River and begin the conquest of the land the LORD your God is ready to hand over to you" (Josh. 1:11 NET).

Joshua knew God promised His people a land that was *bigger*. He promised them a land full of abundance and life. They could not, however, get to this land by staying where they were. Crossing the Jordan into the unknown was an essential for reaching *bigger*. The land was theirs, they could believe it, God had promised it to them, but the journey there was going to be tough. It was going to require great strength, bravery, and careful attention to the Truth. As they marched forward, panic was not an option, because God was with them. He was leading them to *bigger*. Their job was to stay focused and follow.

Just like the Israelites, God has a *bigger* promise for each of us. The change I witnessed in my family, friends, and community and in myself are what led me to believe *bigger* isn't only a word for Yosselin. God really will do more. He really is inviting us into an incredible journey. He really is capable of taking one word and blowing our minds. He is the rebuilder of all things broken and His plans are limitless.

Bigger represents abundance. It represents a place of intimate connectivity where we are drawn to trust Him more than we thought possible. It takes hard work and sacrifice, courage and surrender. It is a life represented in giving way to the Holy Spirit so He can work deeply and gently inside of us, transforming us and moving us closer to who we were created to be. It is a crazy paradox because *bigger* will ultimately bring us the life we are hungry for, but it will, at the same time, cost us the life we currently have.

Everywhere you set foot you are stepping on land you have already been given. Believing *bigger* was for me is what led me to the more abundant places. There is a longing in my heart to know Him in an even more intimate way. I want to live connected to His heart and His Spirit. I want to walk into the unknown trusting in His mighty Name and walking in the fullness of His power.

Bigger is also for you. God wants to do more in your life than you can imagine possible. He has plans for you, plans to give you a hope and a future (Jer. 29:11). No matter where you are in life, regardless the current of the river you stand facing—He is *bigger*. He is a God of *bigger* with *bigger* in store for your faith, *bigger* plans for overcoming your fears and even *bigger* dreams for your future. He wants to work *bigger* in your marriage, *bigger* in your children, and *bigger* in your friendships. He longs to be *bigger*—*bigger* in you and *bigger* through you.

I would like to invite you to join this journey with me. I have been journeying with God toward *bigger* since we met Yosselin and her family; I just didn't recognize it until recently. What I first thought was God doing a mighty work through me, soon became God doing a mighty work in me.

As we journeyed into the unknown for Yosselin, God awakened me to forms of brokenness in my own life I wasn't even aware of. He showed me how my fight for independence sometimes keeps Him at a distance and my need for control limits His power. He showed me the difference in my identity as a servant versus my identity as a friend. He taught me not to fear brokenness, trusting instead that brokenness always presents us with the opportunity for *bigger*. Not just *bigger* for me, but *bigger* for those around me, which ultimately leads to *bigger* for the Kingdom.

As God in me becomes *bigger* to me, He also becomes *bigger* through me. He promises to partner together to bring His Kingdom to earth. If I will allow Him, He will use me to reveal Himself to those around me. As He becomes *bigger* to others, His Kingdom expands. It's His ultimate plan of redemption for His people. As we work on ourselves and surrender to the process of *bigger*, God works on everyone else and the Kingdom grows.

chapter two

Broken? Not Broken?

Sometimes it's hard to see things for what they really are. There are days it takes everything I have to keep my head above water and other days when the worst struggle I have concerns who drank the last Diet Coke or who didn't put the lid back on the toothpaste!

On the hard days, struggling not to go under, I find myself clinging to God and His promises of *bigger* like never before. Other times I am less focused on my struggle and more available to notice the brokenness in the lives of others, like with Yosselin. There are always opportunities in brokenness to be available for others. Recognizing we are broken people, living in a broken world, frees us up to be honest and helpful with one another. Everyone has a story and everyone with a story battles to press forward.

When the personal battles we fight threaten to capsize us, they need our fullest attention. During these times it is okay to use our best energy to keep moving forward. Trying to help people experience what we are not currently experiencing ourselves can either be exhausting or motivating. It's a both/and—we have a responsibility to reach out and help others, but we also have a responsibility to be aware of where we are standing. Believe it or not, we can miss out on experiencing *bigger* by only focusing on the brokenness of others and never taking time to listen to what God might be saying to us directly.

God is multifaceted. He can do a work in and through us, all at the same time. It is in the rhythm of spending intimate time with Him, time in community with others, and time out in the world that we experience *bigger* both in and around us. A relationship exists where we can fully live recognizing and responding to the voice of God on behalf of our own brokenness, while at the same

time recognizing and responding to Him concerning the brokenness of others. Our broken state of being does not disqualify us.
It is often from this place that we serve Him best.

During times of service, we offer up our hearts, knowing they
will be impacted. This is why at the end of a mission trip
we say things like, "They blessed us more than we blessed them."
When we offer our hearts up to help move others toward *bigger*
we have the blessing of being a part of their journey and the crazy
thing is we also experience Jesus as He moves them forward. As
He becomes *bigger* to them, He also becomes *bigger* to us.

PARTNERING WITH THE BROKEN

To be honest with you, I hesitated when we first found out what
was going on with Yosselin. I wanted Yosselin and her family to
get to *bigger*, but I didn't want my family to get hurt on their way
there. My girls had never experienced sickness; they hadn't
known anyone with cancer. Yosselin's diagnosis was compli-
cated and her recovery was going to be extremely difficult. We're
not talking about the flu. She had stage-four osteosarcoma. I
had to live in reality; there was a very real possibility she would
not make it through this battle.

Fearing future pain for my girls almost kept me from surrendering to *bigger*. Choosing to partner with God meant me letting go
of control. My maternal instinct longed for self-preservation and
protection. My initial reaction was to stay in, where it was safe,
rather than step out. I saw no way we could walk beside this family and not be affected by the diagnosis they faced. Their brokenness was going to move us, it was going to challenge us, it was

going to force us outside of our comfort zone and in the end, good or bad, we would be different.

Brokenness leads to *bigger*, even when you think you are not the one broken. Brokenness, when handed over to God, always leads to *bigger*. Serving Him through the broken directly aligns us with His *bigger* purposes. There are only so many walls we can build before our resources run out, our talents cease and, our strength drains. At the end of ourselves we must lean on Him, so we can continue forward. More times than not, I lean too heavily on myself, only to topple over and quit before arriving at *bigger*.

Some of the best *bigger* experiences come on the other side of extending your hand on behalf of someone else's brokenness. My friend Chris is a great example of this. He and his family recently reached out and sponsored a child through the mission organization Back2Back. They sponsor Marcus. Marcus lives in Nigeria. He has limited access to his parents, limited access to education, and what would appear to be a very dim future. The village Marcus lives in is a threat to Marcus's health, simply because it lacks the resources necessary to provide for him.

Marcus lives on the other side of the world, but Chris still stepped up. He reached out and allowed God to build a bridge between him and Marcus. Chris doesn't just send a monthly check in support of Marcus either. He has put his heart out there. He invited Marcus into his family. Marcus's brokenness has now become Chris's brokenness.

In March, I was able to go with Chris and his son, Ethan, to Nigeria, where Ethan would meet Marcus for the first time. Watching these three guys come together was so fun. There was no holding back emotions as they found themselves face-to-face for the very first time. They were family and the bond between them was palpable.

There is heartache when you have to leave part of your family in Nigeria and return to your life in the United States. There is distress when you no longer have instant access to the people you love so much. Chris and Ethan left Nigeria ten days later, with a little bit of heartache. It hurt to separate what God had brought together, but *bigger* proved worth the pain.

NEW PERCEPTIONS

I long to live my life at a place where I no longer fear having my heart broken. Fully understanding *bigger* is on the other side of broken changes the way you look at what's been broken. Does a place exist where I am ready and able to put my heart out there, taking a risk and getting involved in brokenness around me without hesitation, simply because I trust the *bigger?*

Had the outcome for Yosselin been different it would have devastated my family. By committing to walk through the fire with them we realized the possibility of intense pain. We could not control the outcome. But we could trust the One who did. We prayed, we believed and we held on, claiming the *bigger.*

Bigger isn't a one-time thing. It's continual. You don't experience Jesus's healing once and then live the rest of your life based on that one experience. Rather, you are invited to experience it time and time again, as you put your heart out there. There is a lifestyle of continual breakthrough waiting for us.

As a child, my friend was sexually molested by a neighbor. On the other side of her brokenness, God has used her as an advocate for young teenage girls struggling to process the intense emotions following this same type of brokenness. She doesn't hide from the opportunities to embrace these girls. In fact, she seeks them out. She understands God will use her brokenness for His good. He will take the pain in her life and allow it to help others.

Does it hurt as she relives those painful childhood memories? Yes, especially at first, but by this time she has realized the *bigger* is worth the pain. Would she choose to go back and live the nightmare again? No way, but since the brokenness is there she will choose to let it be rebuilt in a way that brings glory to God. God is so good to use our past brokenness to rebuild others.

I have greatly benefited from the brokenness of those around me. Dozens of people have been willing to step into my life and allow their stories and their pain to help me. I am thankful for their vulnerability. They risked the pain of old memories for my benefit. I experienced *bigger*, because they put their hearts on the line.

BRAVE FACES

I made a decision the other day to take off my brave face. I didn't just take it off, I took it off and threw it away. I don't want to live with my brave face on. I want the reality of the pain happening in my life to show for what it really is: pain. The struggle is real and I want to acknowledge it openly. No more living with the mirage of having it all together. He won't fix what we won't admit is broken. What would it look like to live in a world where people openly acknowledge the brokenness in their lives rather than suppressing it in hopes no one noticed?

From a young age we are taught to tough it out, to not show the world our pain and weaknesses. "Living out of the false self creates a compulsive desire to present a perfect image to the public so that everybody will admire us and nobody will know us." [1]

Truth is, we are better off because of our pain and it is only in our weakness we are made strong. There is freedom in living life out loud. There is freedom in coming up from the basement and allowing the warm sun to shine right through your deepest cuts. *Bigger* doesn't happen in the dark.

chapter three

Nehemiah's Bigger

God gave me a gift inside the story of Nehemiah. In this epic story, I found the strength to walk from brokenness to *bigger* over and over again this past year. I do things better with others; having Nehemiah by my side made a difference. Recognizing his sorrow, his heartbreak, and his struggle, as he surrendered to the process of *bigger*, gave me the motivation I needed.

Nehemiah battled for *bigger*. During his battle he was open and honest about the pain, the fear, and the intensity of the work God was asking him to do. In the fire, it is sometimes easy to forget an end is coming. Nehemiah's story reminds us; the *bigger*, in the end, always proves to be worth the battle to get there.

Nehemiah rebuilt the walls around Jerusalem in fifty-two days. Fifty-two days! Not only did he rebuild the walls in fifty-two days, he also restored the hope of God's people, renewed their faith, and rescued their future. Jerusalem was the place God desired to dwell. The Israelites were His chosen people. It was through them He would one day send His Son to present an entirely new plan of redemption to all people, everywhere. This nation was destined to bring the hope of the world into existence, but, for now, it was in ruins.

Nehemiah wasn't afraid of brokenness. Though he was living away from his people and their problems, he invited them in. He allowed their reality to become his reality. Instead of putting up a guard to protect himself from pain, he embraced it. It was in the reality of Israel's brokenness that he received the first glimpses of God's *bigger* intentions.

God used Nehemiah to move His people from a place of destruction, danger, and despair into a place of repair, restoration, and redemption. No matter the situation, we can rest assured, God's plan is always for *bigger*. He never intends to leave us in the broken.

God always positioned me to recognize *bigger*, but without a *bigger* understanding of who He is, it would be impossible to walk in complete freedom. As long as I continued to depend on myself, I would continue to miss out on the adventure waiting.

DEVASTATING NEWS

It's probably safe to say Nehemiah never saw it coming. He wasn't even with God's people when they were freed from captivity and allowed to go back to their broken-down city. Nehemiah was busy being the cupbearer to the king of Persia. He was living his life, minding his own business, when God showed up, out of nowhere, and broke his heart.

Once released from captivity, the Israelites returned to their city, only to realize the walls offering protection from their surrounding enemies had been torn down. With no walls, they would easily fall victim to whoever decided to take advantage of them. With a lack of resources and leadership, there seemed to be no opportunity to rebuild and restore order to this once-vibrant community. Perhaps they were better off as slaves. At least there they had order and protection.

Nehemiah's heart ached for his people, but it is what he did with the pain that made a difference. He partnered with God. He handed the brokenness over and opened himself up to what he could not fully see. Through the process of rebuilding, God proved to be *bigger* than Nehemiah had ever asked or imagined possible. I don't think Nehemiah would have believed it himself had he not been the one walking it out day by day. God wanted to be *bigger* in him and *bigger* through him. God had plans for His people and would go to great lengths to restore what was standing in the way.

A year ago, as I was reading chapter one of Nehemiah in preparation for an upcoming talk, God gave me a glimpse inside the process Nehemiah walked to get to *bigger*. We don't just wake up one day at the *bigger* place. Rather, we surrender to a process. The process involves following plans we don't have the privilege of holding. Instead, the Master builder invites us to journey with Him through the process of rebuilding.

Bigger represents the land we have yet to conquer. It brings on a new understanding of God and the power He holds. It offers deeper intimacy and a supernatural ability to trust what we do not know in the hands of the Almighty. *Bigger* is abundance. It's more of him, more freedom, more identity, more authority, and more power.

Whether he knew it or not, Nehemiah walked this process. He journeyed from brokenness to *bigger*. He cried hard, prayed hard, worked hard, and in the end he experienced more of God than he thought possible. I want to invite you to walk with me from brokenness to *bigger*. No matter how deep or how shallow the place we start, I believe God has more in store for us. On this side of heaven, we will never arrive at the place where He has given us all He has. In the meantime, while we are here, there's always opportunity for *bigger*.

THE PROCESS

Nehemiah did not fear brokenness; instead, he invited it into his life by asking hard questions. He did not allow himself to be overcome by the temptation to fix the wall himself, nor did he ignore the brokenness currently before him. Instead, he sat down and wailed over it. He mourned for days over the state of his people, fasting and praying for God to show up and fix this mess. He reminded God of His promises to His people. He pleaded for Him to intervene.

God will meet us in brokenness. He even reaches out to open the door for us as we start the journey toward *bigger*. The key is walking with Him. We must surrender control and allow Him to lead us. As Nehemiah cried, he also fasted and repented for the idolatry represented in the hearts of his people back home. He repented for not recognizing *bigger* sooner. He pleaded with God for the necessary favor as he moved forward.

Coming out of repentance, Nehemiah turned his back on the current direction his life seemed to be headed as cupbearer to the king and embraced the *bigger* with God. He let go of his need to understand fully and trusted God to do what he could not. He surrendered to the power of prayer as he quietly took those first, scary steps of obedience. He spent time in preparation, abiding in God, recognizing he would need supernatural strength to move the mountain standing in front of him.

When it was time to get to work, he shared the plans, cast the vision God had given him, and called his people. Then he climbed onto his ladder and worked like he had never worked before. Not once did he allow the taunts of the enemy to distract him. He pursued *bigger* for himself and for God's people.

Over and over again he refused to come down off his ladder and stop the work God purposed in his heart to do.

The doors were set in place, a new government in order, and restoration came to God's people once again. It was *bigger, bigger* than they ever imagined possible. God's love for them was deeper than they realized. No matter the role each played in the brokenness, they all celebrated together, in victory. God willingly repaired the damage. In fifty-two days, God, guiding Nehemiah to lead and elicit the help of the people, rebuilt the wall from the rubble it had been. From brokenness to *bigger*.

The most widespread illusion of our day—whether it is said out loud or in our actions—is that we do not need God to do what we do. Nehemiah proves to us that all things are possible when God gets involved. My life changed drastically when I stopped attempting to go it alone and starting clinging to His power. *Bigger* comes slowly when pride keeps us from recognizing God's role in rebuilding.

Won't you take the risk and join me? Invite Him in and see what He sees. Look around and notice what He notices. Take off your mask and allow the pain to be real. *Bigger* exists for you, just like it exists for me. It's time we step forward and claim what is rightfully ours.

Welcome to the *bigger* journey, my friend.

THE BIGGER JOURNEY

chapter four

Hard Questions

The journey toward *bigger* often starts with one hard question. Ella had been coming home for weeks telling me Yosselin was sick. Every single day: "Mom, Yosselin wasn't in school today. Mom, Yosselin was sick again. Mom, do you think something's wrong?"

I ignored her as long as I could. I gave her short answers— "Maybe she's on vacation, Ella " or "Maybe she has the flu"— whatever it took to buy more time.

The truth is, I was terrified to ask what was going on with Yosselin. Not knowing kept me away from the responsibility that came with knowing. Ignorance is bliss, right? I sensed something was wrong and once I knew what it was, I would have a responsibility to do something with it.

Sometimes the hardest part of the journey is recognizing and admitting where we are. It's not easy to admit we are wrong, broken, lost, or better yet, all of the above, but before we can take even one step forward it is essential to acknowledge our own inability to do so without His help.

MOVE ME

I desperately wanted to move forward with God. I knew there was more to life than where I was. I prayed for months asking God to show up and reveal to me who He really was. I noticed the way other people walked with Him, the way they talked with Him, and it was different, more intimate. If there was more to this faith thing, then I wanted in on it. In desperation I cried out and in frustration I waited.

Looking back, I realize He responded almost immediately. I cried out and He answered; I simply ignored it. I didn't like what He said.

Come to me. His plea echoed over and over again in my head and heart. I asked Him to show me something and He offered only to show me Himself. I wanted to do. I wanted to accomplish. I wanted to achieve. He wanted me to be. He didn't want me anywhere but with Him.

Each time I prayed I felt the Spirit whisper in my heart, *Abide in me.* Hearing those words made me quick to defend myself. *I am abiding. Abiding is what I do. I spend my life abiding. Look at the ministry we do, look at these students, look at these women, look at this, look at that.* I defended my abiding by pointing out the fruit hanging all around me. I pleaded my case by devoting more hours to the church. With all that I was doing I was more than a little offended God continued asking me to rest with Him.

Worn out from wrestling with Him, I silently cried, *I just don't get it; I am abiding.* In that still moment I felt Him whisper, *Abide more.*

If the secret to fruitfulness is abiding, then the secret to more fruitfulness is more abiding (John 15). Of course God wanted me to abide more. I wasn't asking Him for fruit, I was asking Him for more fruit. I wasn't asking Him for big, I was asking Him for *bigger*. *Bigger* fruit would take *bigger* abiding. More of Him outside of me meant I first had to experience more of Him inside of me.

Around this time I almost lost my youngest daughter, Addilyn, in the grocery store. I don't remember where we were going, but I remember being in a huge hurry. If I had it to do over again I would have said no to the little cart, but in my rushed state I gave in. At that point the only thing worse than being in a hurry with two small children was being in a hurry with two small, whiny children.

In my rush, I caved and allowed Addilyn to push the little shopping cart through the store. I am convinced that whoever invented those little carts never actually went grocery shopping with a four-year-old, because if they had, they never would have done that to moms all over the country.

As the girls and I made our way through the store, Addy blissfully pushed her little cart, unaware of my ankles and the pain shooting through my legs each time she "forgot to look." At the self-checkout, Ella helped unload the groceries while Addy announced she would put the cart back. I should have looked up, I should have told her no, but my mind was focused on one thing—getting out of the store quickly. I swiped my credit card, grabbed the groceries from Ella, and turned to leave, when I realized Addilyn was no longer with us.

My heart sank as my eyes quickly darted throughout the front of the store, spotting her nowhere. I followed every possible path she could have taken to put the little cart back and still came up empty. She wasn't anywhere. Fear and panic began to take over as I grabbed Ella and ran to the automatic door.

With one foot inside the store and one foot outside the store, I froze. I couldn't decide what to do. What if I went out and she was in? What if I stayed inside and she was out? What if I made the wrong choice and missed her altogether? Those few seconds seemed like an hour as I wrestled with the choice. Go out? Stay in? Go out? Stay in?

Then, out of the corner of my eye I saw her little blonde pony-tail bouncing up and down. She rounded the corner so proud of herself. Like a grown-up, she decided to take the long way to put the cart up. I wanted to cry, hug her, squeeze her, and punish her all at the same time.

STEPPING OUT

Maybe in my desperate search for God I hadn't realized He was asking me to step out of the door, leaving behind the way I knew Him and opening myself up to a new way of knowing him. There was so much He wanted to show me—so much about Him and so much about me. But it all lived outside the door. It was in stepping out into the unknown that I would find what I was looking for. He would meet the growing desires in my heart to know Him more, but I couldn't hold on to the past in fear of letting go.

Abiding more seemed scary. This wasn't my first time around the rodeo. I knew that with abiding came intimacy, with increased intimacy came more opportunities for obedience. Obedience is always costly. It always comes with surrender. In order to hear more of God, I had to hear less of myself. If you know me, you know this to be a struggle.

Abiding more meant submitting to a journey I did not fully understand. I couldn't see the big picture, but I knew where to start. If I was going to learn His voice more intimately it meant

I would have to spend more time with Him. The most practical way to do this was to get up earlier. Getting up earlier seemed fine on paper, but I had one problem.

I had a bad habit of allowing my youngest to crawl in bed with us in the middle of the night. Her warm little body cuddled up next to me in the morning made it really hard to get out of bed. It should be easy to admit having a four-year-old in bed with you is a problem. It wasn't hard for Dave. But I was hooked. I loved it. Addy's my baby. Each night she crawled into my bed, put her chubby little hand on my cheek and drifted back to sleep. I would pull her in close to savor every second. She needed me and I longed to keep it that way. Admitting this was the step God asked me to take was embarrassingly harder than it should have been.

Dave was quick to confirm it was definitely God speaking. He was more than ready to get this precious treasure out of the middle of his bed. We were on completely opposite ends of the spectrum. When Addy climbed in next to me, we drifted back to sleep, dreaming of sunshine and flowers. When she climbed in next to Dave, her perfect little feet made their way to the arch of his back and with an unbelievable force worked to push him out. I couldn't even imagine!

I will never forget the exact moment it became clear to me I was standing in my own way. On a car ride with some of my best friends, our conversation turned to the different things we felt God asking us to do. I sank quietly into the back seat, hoping to go unnoticed. I have good friends and they would never let that happen. With all eyes on me I humbly admitted what God was saying to me, "He has asked me to get Addy out of my bed and get up earlier to be with Him."

It was out there, in the open and other people knew about it. I asked, He answered. I didn't like what He said and tried to ignore it, only to now arrive at the place of repentance. Relief flooded over me.

I am lucky to have friends who refuse to leave me somewhere God doesn't want me. With their encouragement, I recognized my resistance and put a plan in place to move forward.

HARD ANSWERS

I have a habit of avoiding hard questions when I fear not liking the answers. I used to have a no-scale-on-Mondays rule. Monday is a horrible day to weigh in. Weekends are made to enjoy, right? Eat what you want, let go of the workout. A little extra ice cream over here. A lot of pizza over there.

Taking the weekend off makes Monday a hard scale day. I prefer to wait until Tuesday when I have had at least one round at the gym and the calories have had time to spread out a little. Yes! I realize not stepping on the scale doesn't mean the weight is not there. It's still there. I even know it's there! Not acknowledging it enables me to put off dealing with it.

Nehemiah wasn't afraid to ask hard questions. He knew the state of his people in Jerusalem could not be good. They were in captivity for years. Readjusting to the real world was bound to be a struggle. Though he feared the answer, he didn't let his fear keep him from asking. Nehemiah cared more about truth than he did his comfort. Driven by love, Nehemiah was compelled to ask.

Love is what drives *bigger*. Love is what compelled God to provide *bigger*. Love compelled Him to give up His Son so we could have an opportunity for wholeness. Love compels Him to pursue relationship with us. Love compels Him to never give up. Likewise, love compels us to listen and respond to His voice. Nehemiah sacrificed his comfort because of love. He loved God and He loved people.

Hanani told Nehemiah the state of the broken walls. He painted a picture of the devastation God's people were facing and how the exposure left them in a vulnerable position. The neighboring camps could come and go as they please, leaving the Israelites in a dangerous place.

WHAT?

If you don't know where you are, then you can't know where you are going. Dave won't mind me telling you, he's horrible with directions. He would be great, except he gets lost in the excitement of where we are going. In his quest onward he often forgets the reality of where we are.

On our first vacation as a married couple, we learned a valuable lesson: either pay better attention to where you are or listen to your wife! The drive from Cincinnati to Florida was something we both experienced dozens of times growing up. With family in Florida, I felt like I could drive it in my sleep.

Returning home this time was different. Dave, so focused on where we were headed, forgot to pay attention to where we were. He wanted to make it to Georgia. He had to make it to Georgia. No one gets gas in Florida. Gas is cheaper in Georgia. (You can read that in a sarcastic tone if you'd like.) Getting to Georgia became the challenge.

Thirty minutes from the Florida/Georgia line (not the group, the actual place), I pointed out the gas gauge and begged him to admit defeat. Dave was more determined than I was to make it to Georgia. He was confident we could make it. The distance between each exit only grew longer and longer. I will spare you the painful details of the argument ensuing as we pulled our car over to the side of the road, miles from any exit. Big surprise, we were stranded, completely out of gas, on the side of the road, in the middle of nowhere. Our (really Dave's) inability to recognize where we were had cost us.

Every journey has to start somewhere. Let's put aside our fear of asking hard questions and just jump in. Together, let's figure out where we are. Take a minute and ask God, *What's going on?* Before we go any further, pause and ask God to open your eyes to what's going on. I will do it with you.

"Call to me and I will answer you and tell you great and unsearchable things you do not know." (Jer. 33:3).

Maybe try something like this: *God, what's going on? How are things in my life spiritually? Am I who You intended for me to be? Is this bigger? How is my relationship with You? What are the things in our relationship that are keeping me from experiencing bigger? Break my heart over what is not of you in my life.*

> Search me, God, and know my heart; test me and know my anxious thoughts. See if there is any offensive way in me, and lead me in the way everlasting. (Ps. 139:23–24)

There are seasons in life when the answer to what is broken is blatantly obviously: cancer, the loss of someone significant, a job transfer. Then there are other seasons where brokenness can be much harder to recognize: the conviction of pride, a love of money, or deep-rooted idolatry. No matter where you are recognizing it, brokenness is the first step in your journey toward *bigger*.

How did He answer you? Where are you standing? What is He saying?

STRENGTH TRAINING

Developing the ability to hear from God is like developing a muscle. The more we practice, the stronger we become. Using our muscles in new ways is intimidating and often painful at first. Push past the pain. Push past the intimidation. I know God wants to speak to you. I know God has more for you. He will show up when you ask Him to, He promises that.

The first time I lifted weights after having a baby, it felt like my muscles were ripping apart. I was so sore the next day I couldn't sit on the toilet to go to the bathroom. With each step up the stairs I moaned. The second day was even worse.

Why is the soreness of exercise not enough to keep us from going back? Day after day we go back to the very thing causing us pain. We dig deep, we push through. Quitting is not an option because we know the outcome. We know the pain is worth the prize at the end. We push through day after day, week after week, because we know something good is happening on the inside. As we continue to work, our muscles continue to grow. We are building up internal muscle mass that will eventually change our bodies, making us stronger and in better shape.

It's the same with surrender. Sometimes God shows up and shows us really hard things about the reality of where our lives are. Following Him out of those places is costly. The pain from lifting these heavy weights sometimes leads us to second-guess what He is really saying. What if pain were an indicator that it's working? God knows what He is doing. The invitation to *bigger* is an invitation into a process. The process, difficult at times, painful at others, always proves to be worth it in the end.

chapter five

Letting It Go Deep

Bigger has the best beginnings in a place of helplessness. Coming to the end of ourselves leaves us perfectly positioned for the *bigger* things of God. Brokenness does a good job of ending us. It swiftly forces even the most confident person into the unknown. When the walls come down around us, the truth is exposed.

Fear of the truth is often the very thing preventing us from experiencing the *bigger* we were created for. I fear the unknown. I fear the disapproval of those around me and with that comes a colossal fear of failure. I have spent much of my life piecing brokenness back together in the dark. The biggest problem with that— God doesn't fix what we haven't admitted is broken. Truth leads to transformation.

Bigger is a direct result of Truth. We cannot get to *bigger* in the dark. Experiencing the fullness of God in my life means allowing the walls hiding who I am and the life I live to come down and expose truth. For me, it means letting go of the need to appear as though I have it all together. It means fighting to not live for the approval of others. It means a daily surrender of selfish ambition.

LETTING IT BREAK

He might have even wished he could take it back, but it was too late: the look on Hanani's face said it all. It's never easy to let someone in on news you know is going to hurt, but Hanani didn't hide what was going on to protect Nehemiah. He knew if there was any hope for healing and restoration he had to lay it all on the table. The truth was, things were not good. The walls were broken and the future of God's people was uncertain. Without a miracle, the Israelites were doomed to destruction.

"When I heard these things, I sat down and wept" (Neh. 1:4).

Nehemiah's people were in distress. He felt their fear, sensed their insecurities, and understood their shame. He took their brokenness personally, much like God does for us. God takes our pain personally. Our pain is His pain because He carries it for us.

"Surely He took up our pain and bore our suffering" (Isa. 53:4).

Jerusalem was supposed to be God's holy city. It represented Jewish national identity and at one time had been blessed with God's divine presence. Light was destined to come from Jerusalem. God's ultimate plan of redemption was prophesied to come through this city, through these very people. They were ordained to pave the way for the Gentiles, which would, in turn, pave the way for us. Through Jerusalem, people would come to know Jesus. The broken walls stood directly in the way of God's people fulfilling their destiny. Brokenness was keeping them from *bigger*.

Nehemiah's heart was broken, so he sat down and wept. He fought the urge to brush off the pain. He grieved for his people. He grieved for their loss. He grieved over the thought of missing out on *bigger*.

Some people classify weeping as a sign of weakness, but in Nehemiah's case it was a sign of strength. Nehemiah willingly took on a crushing burden. He allowed his heart to be broken. He resisted the urge to control his emotions and instead invited the pain to go deep. He never manipulated the situation or denied it was happening. He simply sat down and had himself a good cry.

It was customary, back in the day, for Jews to sit down while they mourned. The practice of sitting low on the ground was symbolic of the loneliness and depression a mourner felt. Nehemiah followed suit. Instead of pushing past the devastation, he sat down in his brokenness and he wept openly.

SIT DOWN

Sitting down in our weeping enables us to do a few things. First, it keeps us humble. Bowing low is a sign of humility. By bowing to a king, you say that he is greater than you. Sitting now, it is easy to see my pride pushing me to rebuild the walls in my life over the years. My pride wanted to appear different than I was. My arrogance allowed me to blame others and resist the vulnerability of being exposed.

"He leads the humble in what is right, and teaches them his way" (Ps. 25:9).

Pride doesn't work in the *bigger*, because pride is all about us and bigger is all about God. When we allow our brokenness to show for what it is, it keeps us living in a state of humility. My favorite part of our house is the huge windows lining the entire back wall. They face east, which means as soon as the sun is out it is shining brightly through every part of the room. I love it and I hate it, all at the same time. I love the warmth of the sun, how bright and open it is, but I hate that I can't walk out of my bedroom in the morning without shielding my eyes. I hate Saturday mornings, when it is so bright we can't see the television because of the glare and how the sun fully exposes the dust sitting on my bookshelves

When light shines into what's broken it takes time for our eyes to adjust. Pride pushes us to turn the lights back off and keep the truth from being exposed. Pride says we don't need adjustment. But, in order to fully deal with the brokenness, it must be exposed to the Light. God doesn't put things back together in the dark.

Life works better in the light. Spiders live in the dark, that's reason enough for me to avoid it.

> No one lights a lamp and puts it in a place where it will be hidden, or under a bowl. Instead they put it on its stand, so that those who come in may see the light. Your eye is the lamp of your body. When your eyes are healthy, your whole body also is full of light. But when they are unhealthy, your body also is full of darkness. See to it, then, that the light within you is not darkness. Therefore, if your whole body is full of light, and no part of it dark, it will be just as full of light as when a lamp shines its light on you. (Luke 11:33–37)

Jesus desires for us to live exposed lives. Lives open to His light and receptive to healing. The light is not meant to hurt or humiliate, rather it is meant to bring health. The light exposes necessary truth and points us in the direction we must walk. Bigger is dependent on the light.

Sitting in brokenness enables us to see things more clearly. Try this exercise with me: Picture yourself standing; all around you, crumbled at your feet, is your brokenness. Look down at the rubble. Standing over brokenness leaves us in a place of action. It leaves us in control, calling the shots, repairing the damage. The shadow of our posture blocks the sun from fully revealing truth. Now, sit down. Sitting represents a place of surrender. It enables us to look up and invite God into the process.

Sitting gives us time to lift our heads up and look around. Looking around helps us realize we are not alone. We live in a world full of broken people. I am not the only one. You are not the only one. We are not the only ones. We don't have to walk this road alone. Those of us too busy fixing the mess often miss out on the reality of what's going on around us. Something powerful happens when God's people join together in brokenness and wait on Him to move. Taking our eyes off of ourselves and focusing them on Him is essential in this journey. It is in sitting that we best welcome the heart and hands of God.

TODDLERS AND TANTRUMS

I had a love/hate relationship with how willing my girls are to sit down and let the whole world in on what is currently breaking their innocent hearts. I love their purity of not caring who sees they are hurting. At the same time I hate when it happens in the wrong place.

My first reaction is to hide the reckless emotion quickly unfolding. What can I give them? Where's the nearest distraction? The nearest corner? Bathroom? Anything, to duck out of the center aisle. It's late, she's hungry and tired, and that pack of three hundred stickers for one dollar will go a long way to avoid the messiness unfolding in front of me.

As devastating as it is when it happens to you in the middle of the grocery, you have to admit, there is something compelling about the innocence of not caring who is watching. As children we spent countless hours not caring who saw us melting. But as adults we quickly wipe the tears, straighten our jackets, and walk forward, praying no one noticed.

We have been conditioned to do what it takes to hide the brokenness inside of us. We hide pain. We hide emotion. We hide hurt. We hide anger, resentment, and even jealousy. We hide behind text messages and computer screens. We hide behind relationships, demanding jobs, and countless activities. We get into the car a mess, argue all the way to the soccer field, the dance studio, the dinner reservation, or even the church and then somehow get out with it all together.

PICTURE PERFECT

Backing out of our driveway the other day I slammed the back of my car into the front of Dave's trailer, leaving a gaping hole in the bumper of my Saturn Vue. I got out of the car and looked at Dave. "I didn't see it," I confessed. It was the truth; I didn't see. Of course, I was in a huge hurry and I wasn't really looking. The worst part: we were supposed to be on our way to have our family pictures taken. Our time crunch left no time to dwell on the accident.

Dave fought to hold back his frustration. I could see numbers running through his head as he added the cost of replacing the bumper to the monthly budget. "Say something," I said as we pulled back out of the driveway.

"What do you want me to say?" he asked, annoyed.

"I don't know; tell me it's okay."

"It's okay," he said, biting his tongue and trying to play the loving, supportive husband role.

There we were, all four of us, in our perfectly coordinated outfits, driving to have our family pictures taken, ready to kill each other. All morning I nagged Dave to hurry up. All morning my girls fought. All morning I rushed. And now, in my rush, I wrecked the car. I was on edge, Dave was on edge and both the girls were spent. You could cut the tension with a knife.

Addy started crying. Ella jumped to my defense. I issued a call for silence. Since no one, including myself, had anything good to say, we would ride to family pictures silently. Getting out of the car I shot a sideways look to Dave and muttered under my breath, "Perfect, now that we are all so happy with one another, let's go take family pictures!"

No part of me wanted to be joyfully posing for pictures that morning. I wanted my Victoria's Secret sweats, a fresh cup of coffee, and a new start. Instead, here I was with an hour photo session, smiling, hugging and high-fiving the people who I just threatened to leave on the side of the road if they talked.

I value authenticity. It's a natural side effect of growing up in a world of secrets. Wasted years sitting in the dark have left me with a need to be real. I choose to struggle out in the open. I am breaking the cycle in my family. Brokenness is not best kept in secret. I desperately want to pass the value of authenticity down to my girls—so much so that having inauthentic moments weighs heavy on me. I don't want to be something I'm not. I don't want to appear one way and live another, even for a second. Pretending gets you nowhere.

Hiding our brokenness only pushes the root cause to the side. Sweeping pain under the rug leaves it under the rug, and under the rug, it never gets dealt with.

Living in secret makes me a recovering fix-a-holic. Basically, I have made a life of bandaging up what's broken. I have become so good at bandaging things, I could do it in my sleep. I can bandage up pride and make it appear humble. I can bandage up fear and make it appear courageous. I can bandage up anger and make it feel like love. Hiding what's broken has been a large part of my life and I'm not proud to say I think I was getting pretty good at it.

There's one problem with those bandages: they don't hold forever. It's the truth about bandages, if you splurge and buy the expensive ones, they may hold up through a rainstorm, but eventually the stickiness wears off, leaving your open wound fully exposed.

Bandages keep us living with a false sense of wholeness. They keep us in the dark, away from the *bigger*. Allowing the walls to come down in our lives gives God the access He needs to lead us in rebuilding. With God rebuilding, there is simply no need for bandages. What He builds will never be undone.

Steph didn't ask for her dad to be a drug dealer, nor did she ask for her mom to move random guys into their house throughout her teenage years. She could have hidden in her brokenness, protecting herself from the judgment of the world. Instead, she invited people in. She exposed the truth of her life and cried out for help. God heard her cries. He picked her up and placed her in a church family that could love her into the *bigger*. God didn't cause her brokenness, but He intended to rebuild it for her good.

Seven years ago, as Dave and I worked to move seventeen-year-old Steph into our house, none of us could make sense out of the brokenness in her life. Without fully understanding, she surrendered to the process. She wept openly and allowed God to begin a work of healing in her that would eventually take her to *bigger*. On the other side of brokenness, she still aches over her childhood disappointments, but she greatly rejoices over the intimacy she found with her rebuilder. She rejoices over the story unfolding and the redemption she's experienced.

It is in our brokenness we are most opened to God, because it is there He has complete access. At no other time are the walls of our lives down, leaving us vulnerable to the Master's hands. In this place of vulnerability, we are able to rely on someone other than ourselves. God is in the business of rebuilding what's been broken, but He refuses to do it with Band-Aids. If we are patient, He will help us rebuild, one brick at a time, moving us from a place of brokenness to *bigger*. Brokenness always leads to *bigger* when put in the hands of the ultimate rebuilder.

As I sit here typing, I am on the verge of tears. My family is in the midst of extreme heartbreak. It is one thing to experience heartbreak of your own, but it is entirely different to watch your loved ones experience heartbreak you can do nothing about. It feels helpless and isolating. In the past, I have been the rebuilder, working quickly to rebuild the walls of the people I love most in order to keep out what I saw as unnecessary pain.

This time, however, something feels different. In my quest to experience more of Him, I feel the Holy Spirit asking me to sit in my brokenness. I feel conviction over the times I robbed my family of the *bigger* rebuilding process of God, because it hurt me too much to watch their pain.

WALK IT OUT

Nehemiah has taught me to walk out brokenness differently. If *bigger* exists for everyone and brokenness leads to *bigger*, then the brokenness of the ones I love the most is the very thing that will lead them to the *bigger* I so desperately want them to find. I want them to know God and to experience His undying love for them. I want them to trust Him and to learn to hear His sweet, soft voice. I want them to experience the intimacy developed at He works to rebuild.

I am no longer interested in my family experiencing the rebuilding process of Kristan. I am not the answer. I don't know the answer, but I know who does. Instead of walking with me, I want them to walk with Jesus. Together, one brick at a time, He will help them put the pieces exactly where they need to go. He has the blueprints. He sees the big picture.

BIRTHING THE IMPOSSIBLE

Pregnancy and I are not friends. I promise you, this is not an exaggeration, ask anyone who knows me, they will tell you it's true. They will tell you I threw up every morning for seven months, and just in case that wasn't enough, I threw up every night also. By the time I was four months pregnant, my feet were so swollen I could only wear one pair of shoes. It wasn't pretty and I rejoice that this part of my life is over!

However, I would do it one hundred times over again to have my two girls. I promise, I would. I'm head over heels in love with them. A love I didn't know I was capable of experiencing. In a matter of seconds, I loved these little babies so much I would do anything for them, even if it meant giving my own life. I rejoice in them, I smile over them; I sing over them. They are my life, my precious treasures.

Sometimes, it's hard for me to believe God loves me as much as He says He does. I am so unworthy. I have done nothing to earn it, nothing to deserve it. On those days, I fight to remember the first minute holding my baby girls. There's simply nothing like it. His love is overwhelming. A love that intense doesn't leave someone sitting alone in brokenness.

God loves you. He loves you in your mess. He loves you **with** your mess. He loves you, **in spite of** your mess. He loves you so much He refuses to leave you where you are. His heart is to meet you in what's broken and lead you out.

"He heals the brokenhearted and binds up their wounds" (Ps.147:3).

Recently, Ella had her feelings hurt by one of her best friends, and even though I saw where the misunderstanding was coming from, my heart was broken because of her tears. Her little nine-year-old heart hurt, which made my heart hurt. That night, as she struggled to fall asleep, I would have given anything to be able to erase the memory of what happened and bind her pain, but I couldn't. I couldn't change what already happened, but I could sit with her. I could pull her in close and hold her while she cried.

God's heart breaks when our hearts break. If we will allow Him, He will join us in heartbreak. He will pull us in close and He will even carry our pain. God doesn't expect us to cover it up.

Sitting puts us in a place of surrender.

Sitting invites Him in.

chapter six

Believing in Bigger

Remember the first time you had your heart broken? How could you forget, right? I remember mine; I was a junior in high school and head over heels for the guy I was dating. Ten or eleven months into our exclusive relationship, I learned it was not so exclusive to him. As if the news of his cheating ways weren't heartbreaking enough, I discovered the girl he was secretly spending all of his free time with was one of my very best friends, or so I thought!

At the time, I didn't know my heart could ache so badly. To be hurt by a guy was one thing, but the betrayal by my best friend took things to an entirely different level. What was she thinking? It hurt so badly I couldn't eat, I couldn't sleep, I couldn't even think straight. For a while, the heartbreak affected everything I did. It was hard to be at school, harder to be at basketball practice, and even harder to hang out with my friends on the weekend. As a teenager, I was feeling heartbroken in a way I hadn't known existed.

Unfortunately, that wasn't the last heartbreak I would walk through. It even seems silly now, having lived life a little longer. Life brings heartbreak, plain and simple. It can't be avoided. Inevitably it will happen.

PLAY WITH YOUR WHOLE HEART

Growing up, I had a soccer coach who paced frantically up and down the sidelines, yelling at us to play with more heart. His face was as red as the red card the refs often threatened him with. To play with heart implies putting everything on the line. It's getting all the way in and not turning back. If we were going to lose the game, then our coach wanted us to go down swinging. No regrets.

I'm not surprised that we didn't lose many games. After the games we did lose, I walked off the field, crying over the heartbreaking defeat. Putting it all out there doesn't ensure you won't get hurt. Losing the game hurt, but losing without trying would have hurt worse.

What enjoyment would life bring if we never put our hearts on the line? If we only ever got halfway in, playing hesitantly, if at all.

My best friend, Angie, just had a baby. He's beautiful and absolutely perfect in every way. It's hard to remember there were moments we thought he wouldn't be here. Just weeks into her third pregnancy we sat on her living room floor crying out to Jesus for a miracle. Angie was bleeding, profusely. The doctor prepared her for the worst. It was most likely a miscarriage. Having been down this road with a previous pregnancy, she was well aware of the approaching pain. From the outside I could see her struggle: put it all on the line and expect the miracle or protect the heart and prepare for the worst?

Weeks passed as her appointment approached and I'm proud to say she got all the way in. She fought the urge to build walls of protection around her heart and claimed the miracle. She didn't hold back. She prayed, she hoped, and she believed.

Sometimes I catch myself holding back as a way of protecting myself. But pain is pain. Heartbreak hurts, no matter the cause. Why not just put it all on the line? Why not get all the way in? Why not allow your heart to break intensely over whatever pain is in front of you? God is *bigger* than heartbreak and what He rebuilds never crumbles.

NEHEMIAH'S HEARTBREAK

Nehemiah loved. He loved his God and he loved his people. He loved his homeland and now, because of his love, his heart was broken. The devastating news concerning the state of the Israelites left him sitting in pain, crying out to God. As he sat, weeping and wailing, he began to recognize something. He wasn't alone. Sitting in brokenness puts us near the heart of God.

"The LORD is near the brokenhearted" (Ps. 34:18 NET).

In Nehemiah's brokenness, God came near. As He stood near, He enabled Nehemiah to see His heart. He lifted Nehemiah's eyes off the cause of brokenness and showed him the way forward.

Outrageous things happen when we connect with God in brokenness. For Nehemiah, connecting enabled him to realize God was fully aware of the trouble in Jerusalem. He was aware and He wasn't worried. The Israelites might have been panicked, but He wasn't. Our God doesn't panic. He had a plan.

God's heart ached for His people as He watched them stand over their brokenness. He drew near and waited for them. They were His people. He chose them. He fathered them. The plans He had in mind were big plans. He longed to lead them to *bigger*. God's plans didn't change simply because something was broken. His plan was *bigger* than brokenness.

BROKENNESS IN THE BIBLE

It's the story woven all throughout the Bible. It's His story, the story of God meeting us where we are and leading us to the place He intends for us to be. We see it over and over again, with multiple people, in multiple ways.

Jairus was a synagogue ruler. This meant, even though he had probably witnessed some of Jesus's miracles, he would still have had a hard time calling Jesus the Messiah. Then one day, brokenness hit too close to home and everything changed. Jairus's twelve-year-old daughter was dying. He was desperate. Being a synagogue ruler, he spent a large part of his day fixing things, but he could not fix his daughter. He could not overcome death. As his world came crashing down around him, he ran to Jesus. In his desperation, he cried out for Jesus to fix the broken.

❧

Maybe the sinful woman didn't even notice her brokenness anymore. But her brokenness noticed her. Her brokenness knew her name and called her by it, often. At some point it seemed they even become friends. Perhaps they are better together. This is the hand they have been dealt.

If we are not careful there comes a point when we become so accustomed to what's broken, we stop noticing it all together. Brokenness had become who she was, but Jesus didn't see her that way. He was too busy seeing her for who she could be. He recognized how those in her community rejected her. He recognized her avoiding them at all cost.

Her brokenness didn't scare Him. He sat with her in it and even offered to help piece it back together. He offered her new life. As He talked, something inside of her burned. Her perspective began to change and she wondered, *Could what this man is saying be true? Could I really receive healing from this pain? Do I really get a bigger?*

The hemorrhaging woman had been an outcast for twelve years. Her brokenness forced her to live on the outside of her community. She had a disease she didn't ask for, and it cost her everything. She wasn't even welcomed into the Temple to worship. Anyone she touched would be unclean, and so she touched no one. Lost and alone for years, she tried to find help. Spending all her money on doctors who could do nothing for her, she found herself out of options. In her brokenness, she recognized the power of the Messiah. She knew if she could just touch Him, He would heal her. She knew He was her only hope. He was the answer she had been seeking. He was her rebuilder and getting to Him was absolutely necessary.

Zacchaeus was a tax collector. He was a wealthy man, which meant he was good at what he did. He robbed the people to benefit the government and himself. Everyone hated Zacchaeus. They hated him for what he took from them. They hated how he profited off of their vulnerability. When he met Jesus, his eyes were opened to the brokenness in his life. For the first time, he saw his sin for what it really was. He saw his choices and how they hurt those around him. He saw his selfishness. He saw who he had become. That evening as Jesus ate with him, Zaccheaus's perspective changed.

Brokenness always leads to *bigger* when we hand it over to Jesus. We are not equipped to put the pieces back together. We were not meant to step over the rubble and ignore it either. We serve a God who is ready and able to take that which is broken in our lives and work it out for *bigger*. On the other side of our brokenness, we have a bigger understanding of who He is. On the other side of our brokenness, we have a *bigger* faith in what He can do. On the other side of our brokenness, we have a *bigger* ability to face the future.

My tears in the past six months have represented so much more than sadness. They have represented me coming to the end of myself and beginning to recognize God's invitation into *bigger*. I quickly learned *bigger* would come on the other side of admitting the broken and surrendering to the process of transformation.

PADDLES, RAPIDS, ROCKS AND CANOES

I swore I would never canoe again. To say I do not thrive in nature would be putting it lightly. But here I was, somehow organizing a canoe experience for over eight hundred students and of course, my team felt it would be impossible to organize the trip, without experiencing it ourselves first.

The objective of the experience was to hear God's voice in nature. You could say my rowing partner, Dana, and I were good at canoeing because we sure did work harder than anyone else on the water that day. But the harder we worked, the further behind we fell. Instead of paddling downstream like the rest of the team, we struggled, going from one side of the river to the other, for hours.

We lacked the rhythm needed to thrive with the current of the river. I paddled too hard. She paddled too soft. I steered one way, she steered the other. We knew what we were supposed to do and tried our best to do it, but it simply wasn't happening.

Until one of our other teammates, an experienced kayaker, suggested we stop trying so hard. "It just seems like you're forcing it. Can you just stop paddling so intently and allow the river to carry you downstream?" Sounds like a simple enough question, right? "Sit still and see what happens." Desperate for anything, we put our paddles on our laps and watched in amazement, as our canoe began to float downstream carried effortlessly by the current.

In that moment, even in nature, I felt my heart connect with the heart of God and I heard what I believe He was saying to us, *Stop forcing it, stop trying to work so hard and allow it to just be. I will take you forward; just sit back and let me do what I do.*

My inability to control my canoe left me defeated. Victory came the moment I placed the oars on my lap and allowed the natural current of the river to carry me downstream. Likewise, as I fight against what's broken in my life I often feel out of control and defeated. Victory comes when I lay my fight down and let God lead me on the journey toward *bigger*. It is always in surrender I find victory and peace, even on the hardest days.

I fought against the brokenness in my family for years. From the time I was a teenager, I remember putting pieces of the wall back together—pieces I had no business even holding, let alone rebuilding. I remember sitting at the dinner table with close family members, tears streaming down my face, Bible in one hand, Kleenexes in the other, desperately trying to rebuild what had been broken. I refused to go down without a fight, even if it wasn't my fight to fight.

Paddling through the waters that afternoon, God taught me a powerful lesson. I am not and never have been in control. Fighting to play a role that does not belong to me will only keep me struggling. I can fight or I can float. Either way I end at the same place. I am at my best when I put my oars down and learn to float in rhythm with His current.

Do you trust Him enough to put your oars down? Do you trust His ability to lead you out of what's broken? Do you trust His motives? Do you trust Him more than your closest family or best friends? God has a plan for you and it starts with allowing Him access to the broken.

DON'T PANIC

I recognize myself in actions of the Israelites in Exodus 14. Their cries reached God and He was in the middle of answering them, when they freaked out. Moses had gone before Pharaoh demanding he let God's people go. It took a little convincing, but God eventually softened Pharaoh's heart toward His people, causing him to release the captives. As the Israelites approached freedom, it actually says, the Lord hardened Pharaoh's heart, causing him to pursue the Israelites who were marching boldly out of Egypt (Exod. 14:8).

The will of God was not for the Israelites to get to freedom on their own initiative. God already had a redemptive plan in place. There was no need for them to be in control. There was also no need for panic. God's plan was not their plan. He wanted His people to know who it was rescuing them from slavery.

As they journeyed toward freedom Pharaoh changed his mind. What was he thinking—he wasn't ready to release his slaves. He needed them. They were his. Who would do all of the work without them? As his anger grew, he loaded up his army and rushed out of Egypt to take back what was rightfully his.

As Pharaoh's army closed in on the Israelites, they panicked. In their panic, they forgot about *bigger*. They forgot all God had done in front of them and only focused on the rubble lying directly around them. They took their eyes off of the one leading the way and let fear overtake them. Terrified, they turned on Moses.

> "Was it because there were no graves in Egypt that you brought us to the desert to die? What have you done to us by bringing us out of Egypt? Didn't we say to you in Egypt, 'Leave us alone; let us serve the Egyptians'? It would have been better for us to serve the Egyptians than to die in the desert!"

> Moses answered the people, "Do not be afraid. Stand firm and you will see the deliverance the LORD will bring you today. The Egyptians you see today you will never see again. The Lord will fight for you; you need only to be still." (Exod. 14:11–14)

God doesn't need us to panic over what's broken. He's got it. Our brokenness doesn't intimidate him. He is fully capable of putting the pieces back together. We don't have to worry; He can handle our biggest problems, our biggest failures, and our biggest fears.

Letting go of control is scary. Taking our hands off takes trust. The enemy uses fear to keep us controlling that which we were not meant to control. *Bigger* doesn't come in panic. Sitting in a canoe, turning in circles, we give up and throw in the oars thinking it's over and we've lost. However, it is in the losing, we actually win. It is in calm surrender that we can best move forward and experience *bigger*.

"If you cling to your life, you will lose it, and if you let your life go, you will save it" (Luke 17:33 NLT).

What is broken in your life right now? You would have no need for Jesus if something weren't broken. What is it you cling to? What do you fear? What are you struggling to trust Him with? Brokenness isn't always our choice, but what we do with it is. When we allow ourselves to be broken and choose to remain open before God, we always find ourselves positioned for *bigger*.

"Submit yourselves, then, to God. Resist the devil, and he will flee from you. Come near to God and he will come near to you. Wash your hands, you sinners, and purify your hearts, you double-minded. Grieve, mourn and wail. Change your laughter to mourning and your joy to gloom. Humble yourselves before the Lord, and he will lift you up." (James 4:7-10).

Invite heartbreak in. Ask hard questions. Listen to the answers. Sit down and weep over the state of what's broken. Allow it to go deep. Fight the urge to panic. Go with it. He will meet you there. He stands behind you. He weeps with you. He promises to take you to bigger.

THE PROCESS

chapter seven

Bigger Prayers

Sometimes, don't you just need a moment? Yesterday, my youngest, Addy, flipped. She completely lost it. My best friend, Angie was over with her daughter, Addison, and the two of them were having so much fun playing that the mere mention of Addison leaving led to a massive breakdown. In a fit of tears, Addy stormed to her room, slammed the door, and wailed into her pillow. I tried negotiating with her through the door, but quickly realized her ability to reason had gone out the window. Quietly, I walked back downstairs and allowed her the space to have her moment.

As I packed my friend up to leave, I heard Addy tiptoeing around upstairs. We had no more than walked outside and rounded the corner toward the driveway when she burst out the front door. She took a deep breath and embraced her best friend in this huge, *I love you so much it hurts*, hug. They said bye and it was over, just like that. Her moment ended, almost as quickly as it began. She was on the other side and able to see more clearly.

It was intense while it lasted. Some would say unnecessary, but the moment didn't bother me because it allowed her to get to where she needed to be. Had she chosen to stay in the moment, then we would have an issue, but she didn't. She turned around and embraced reality: her friend was going home, playtime was over, and life would soon go on.

NEHEMIAH'S MOMENT

God's people were facing destruction. With the walls of Jerusalem down, it was simply a matter of time before the surrounding enemies took full advantage of their weak position. Nehemiah's heart ached for what was happening back home and his response sends a powerful message, "For some days I mourned and fasted and prayed before the God of heaven" (Neh. 1:4).

Nehemiah had his moment. He allowed the pain of heartbreak to go deep. So deep that the heaviness of it forced him to sit down. For years I fought to not bother God with my moments. There are far too many things going on for Him to have to deal with my fit. I didn't want to be in the way. God can handle our moments. He can handle our weeping and wailing. He is equipped to deal with our dismay. He sees the pain. He understands the shock and patiently waits behind the door, giving us the time necessary for it to go deep. Sometimes brokenness knocks the wind out of us in a way that forces us to sit down.

The other day, I received a devastating phone call. My mouth went numb as I struggled to find the appropriate words to say. The end of a marriage is never easy to accept, especially when it comes out of nowhere. My heart broke into a million pieces. It was unexpected, which left me unprepared. From the outside, everything seemed fine, but under the radar, there had been an intense struggle in brokenness for years.

Sitting on the cold tile floor of my bathroom, I cried. Picturing the new reality of an unknown future crushed my spirit. I wept, imaging the years of pain. I wept because I felt helpless. I wept because this wasn't supposed to happen. Not like this. Bigger doesn't give up.

If we fight the urge to give up in brokenness and instead hand it over to God, He promises brokenness eventually leads to *bigger*— even when it feels impossible, even when it seems as though it is taking forever, even when the whole world looks to be against you. No matter what, if we will trust Jesus, brokenness always leads to *bigger*. God's ability doesn't run out simply because our ability to keep trying wanes. Weary moments are the moments we must cling to Him even more. Those are the moments we cannot lose sight of *bigger*. Our faith in His promises will empower us to keep moving.

I tried calling my best friend, but when she picked up I couldn't get the painful words out of my mouth. I ached for the pain people I loved were facing.

The trajectory of our lives swiftly changed and we struggled to keep our heads above water. Sometimes we battle outside sources we have no control over. In those battles we must learn daily to rely on the only One capable of rebuilding after destruction.

I no longer fight the urge to hide my brokenness. I am confident God can handle my vulnerable reactions to the pain in my life. He can handle them, but He does not intend to leave me sitting in such brokenness long. I don't pretend to know what the future looks like for my family, but I know we have one. I know we have hope. I know healing and restoration will come our way as we surrender to the rebuilding plans of the Master builder.

FIGHT OR FLIGHT

When the initial pain of heartbreak hits, we react. If we let Him, God will take our reactions and turn them into responses. His grace is sufficient. He promises to supply us with what we need to move forward. Life is absolutely not fair. The unexpected and unplanned definitely will happen. We live in a broken and fallen world but we do not serve a broken God. Trying to make sense of the brokenness often leaves us walking in circles.

I have learned it's okay to sit down and let it all out. I'll take my moment, but somewhere in the midst of that moment, I must turn my cries away from the rubble surrounding me and turn them toward the God who stands over me.

My cries of pain must double as prayers to God because He aches with me.

"In the same way, the Spirit helps us in our weakness. We do not know what we ought to pray for, but the Spirit himself intercedes for us through wordless groans" (Rom. 8:26).

When my heart hurts, His heart hurts. When I don't have the words, He provides them for me. He will wait with me in the dark places, but He also reaches into the darkness and offers to carry me out. He is the only one who knows how the pieces go back together in a way more perfect than before. He has the faith I need to get up off the floor and walk forward.

Nehemiah didn't care who saw him. He didn't waste any time worrying about who would notice. He sat down, right in the middle of brokenness, and wept openly before God. Taking full advantage of his moment, he allowed the heartbreak to go deep. But, then his cries turned to prayers. In desperation he cried out to God. The weight of the pain pushed him to his knees. Praying in the midst of heartbreak changes everything. It takes what we don't understand and lines it up with a God who fully understands.

MOVE ME

It's common to think our prayers are for God and somehow represent our feeble attempt to invite Him into what's broken. The truth couldn't be more opposite, although God loves to be invited into things, rest assured, He's already there. He stands right behind you, weeping with you. Our prayers change things because our prayers change us. The prayers we pray move God, but in my experience, they move us more. Over the course of time, our prayers change us, challenge us, and grow us. Connecting with Him gives us the strength needed to lift our eyes off of the broken. Our prayers align us to bigger.

"Prayers are prophecies. They are the best predictors of your spiritual future. Who you become is determined by how you pray. Ultimately, the transcript of your prayers becomes the script of your life." [2]

In Nehemiah's brokenness, he didn't call a town meeting, he didn't run to his closest friends, nor did he hide under his bed pretending it wasn't happening. He cried out to God. He sat before the throne and poured his heart out. Read Nehemiah's:

> LORD, the God of heaven, the great and awesome God, who keeps his covenant of love with those who love him and keep his commandments, let your ear be attentive and your eyes open to hear the prayer your servant is praying before you day and night for your servants, the people of Israel. I confess the sins we Israelites, including myself and my father's family, have committed against you. We have acted very wickedly toward you. We have not obeyed the commands, decrees and laws you gave your servant Moses.

Remember the instruction you gave your servant Moses, saying, 'If you are unfaithful, I will scatter you among the nations, but if you return to me and obey my commands, then even if your exiled people are at the farthest horizon, I will gather them from there and bring them to the place I have chosen as a dwelling for my Name.' They are your servants and your people, whom you redeemed by your great strength and your mighty hand. Lord, let your ear be attentive to the prayer of this your servant and to the prayer of your servants who delight in revering your name. Give your servant success today by granting him favor in the presence of this man. (Neh. 1:5-11)

These verses serve as a summary of how Nehemiah petitioned God both day and night for several months. He leaned on the liturgical traditions he more than likely learned as a child and came intentionally before God. He recognized God was bigger than the brokenness he faced. Nehemiah's prayer provides us with a model of how to find God in brokenness. Whether it's our brokenness or the brokenness of someone around us, prayer is always the first step in the journey toward *bigger*.

PRAISE HIS AWESOMENESS

Nehemiah recognized the immensity of the God he served and even in brokenness he acknowledged it. Notice the way he addresses God, "Lord (*Yahweh*), God of Heaven, the great and awesome God" (Neh. 1:5). *Yahweh* was the name God gave Himself. It is a name based in love, His love for His people. *Yahweh* was Nehemiah's way of recognizing God's love in his life. This broken situation didn't change the love He knew God had for him.

"God of heaven"(Neh. 1:5).

We do not serve a God bound to this earth. God is not limited in the ways we are limited. He is grand; He is mighty and can do whatever He pleases. We can come to Him because He is *Yahweh*, our God of love. We count on Him because He is Yahweh, our God of heaven. No doubt Nehemiah struggled in his pain. But his prayers served as a faithful reminder of the *bigger* God standing over him.

Addy loves to play soccer. She's five, so what she knows of soccer is less than impressive, but I am confident in her ability to get there. One day she'll be playing under the lights, surrounded by cheering fans (or at least grandparents) and loving every second of it. Growing up as an avid soccer player, I cannot wait to be a soccer mom. The excitement of team spaghetti dinners, tournament trips, and two-a-day trainings makes my heart skip a beat! Right now though, I am enjoying the look on Addy's face when I impress her–especially since my skills are more than a little rusty. She watches me dribble. She notes how I juggle, how I kick, and even the soccer language I speak in. I remember what it was like to be a little girl soccer player with a big dream.

As a little girl, I loved going to my hometown's high school varsity soccer games. I wanted to be just like the players on the field. They seemed untouchable. I memorized their every move. I knew their names, positions, and even numbers. I could tell you the leading scorer, what opponents they would struggle to beat, and their potential to be seeded in the seasonal tournament. I would have given anything to have time in their presence, because to me they were larger than life.

We serve a God who is so much more impressive than my washed-up soccer skills. Isaiah 40:26 says, "Lift up your eyes and look to the heavens: Who created all these? He who brings out the starry host one by one and calls forth each of them by name. Because of his great power and mighty strength, not one of them is missing

God does not lack in awesomeness, we lack in noticing His awesomeness.

Even in the midst of tremendous pain, Nehemiah remembered how magnificent God was. It is easy to recognize the awesomeness of God in victory, but it is *necessary* to recognize it in heartbreak. Are you having a hard time recognizing God's awesomeness? Does His righteousness seem far from what you are weeping over? Pray it anyway. Cry, weep, wail, whatever it takes, just do it directed toward Him. Our prayers to God in these moments will not return to us void. He will always be *bigger* than what you face.

CONFESS OUR UNWORTHINESS

The next part of Nehemiah's prayer was confession. He confessed his sins and the sins of his people. Nehemiah recognized Israel's sin and associated himself with his people. Not living there, it would have been easy for Nehemiah to blame the Israelites for their current state of being. Nehemiah raises the bar; their problems are his problems because they affect the future of the Kingdom.

Other people's sin, what's broken in the lives of those surrounding us, is never larger than our own. It's simply different.

Spending all of our time separating and blaming only leaves all of us missing out on the *bigger* God intends. No matter how bad our pain, we are not against one another. We are in this together.

"There is no one righteous, not even one; there is no one who understands; there is no one who seeks God. All have turned away, they have together become worthless; there is no one who does good, not even one" (Rom. 3:10–12).

Can we all agree no one is perfect? Can we admit we have all played a role in the brokenness surrounding us at some point in time? Nehemiah could have easily shaken his head and blamed the Israelites for the position they were in. They were the ones who turned against God. They were the ones who doubted. Sin, regardless of whose it is and how it happened, always robs from *bigger*.

We live in a world where the truth has been distorted; the path has been corrupted and right is often in the eye of the beholder. There are not always answers. Stop blaming and just be sorry. As you sit in brokenness, crying, look up and notice the broken-down walls all around you and just be sorry. Be sorry we are a people guilty of trying to do this on our own.

CLAIM HIS PROMISES

Moving away from the need to blame enables us to better see the promises of God. When Nehemiah lifted his head, he noticed the brokenness all around him and he began to remind God of His promises. "Remember the instruction you gave your servant Moses, saying, 'If you are unfaithful, I will scatter you among the nations, but if you return to me and obey my commands, then even if your exiled people are at the farthest horizon, I will gather them from there and bring them to the place I have chosen as a dwelling for my Name'" (Neh. 1:8-9).

God's promises to us are true. "Trust in the LORD with all your heart and lean not on your own understanding; in all your ways submit to him, and he will make your paths straight" (Prov. 3:5-6).

"Come to me, all you who are weary and burdened, and I will give you rest. Take my yoke upon you and learn from me, for I am gentle and humble in heart, and you will find rest for your souls" (Matt. 11:28-29).

"He gives strength to the weary and increases the power of the weak" (Isa. 40:29).

"And my God will meet all your needs according to the riches of his glory in Christ Jesus" (Phil. 4:19).

I could keep going, because there is a promise for everything. Proclaiming His promises is one of the most powerful prayers you can pray. Confess your need to believe *bigger*.

Focused on the promises of God, Nehemiah found the strength to begin conversation about moving forward. There is a time to sit and a time to move. As you sit before the Lord in prayer and fasting, know movement is coming. God is a God of movement. From the very beginning, He created us to be productive people. If you are calling out to Him, He will answer you. When He answers, be ready to move. He never intends to leave us where we are.

Movement without God is foolish. So often we work and then ask for His blessing, but what if we asked for His blessing and then worked? What if we stopped focusing on the why and started focusing on the Who? Nehemiah asked for God's blessing. He saw the reason His people were in brokenness, but chose to focus on the promises of God instead. Staying focused on the promises of God enabled him to recognize the necessity of moving forward.

On my own, I needed to make sense of my pain. On my own, I needed to understand fully how we arrived at this place of brokenness. On my own, I needed justice for the time lost, the dreams shattered, the hours spent sitting in hurt and wrestling with unbelief. On my own, I walked in circles, and if left on my own, I will continue to walk in circles. It is when I surrender my hurt that I find the help I need.

"It is for freedom that Christ has set us free. Stand firm, then, and do not let yourself be burdened again by a yoke of slavery" (Gal. 5:1). Christ came so we could be free from burdens. When life feels heavy I wonder who is carrying my load, Him or me. When the brokenness of those around me offends me, it is probably safe to say I carry a load that is not mine. The promise in my brokenness is I serve a God ready and waiting to carry me out.

WALKING OUT

I'm walking out. It's hard; it's painful. There are days I move forward and other days I am dizzy from walking in circles. On the hard days I remind myself, I don't need to see, I don't need to understand, I just need to trust. "Surely God is my salvation; I will trust and not be afraid. The LORD, the LORD himself, is my strength and my defense; he has become my salvation" (Isa. 12:2). Step by step, He helps me carry my load. As we walk, I grow. As we walk, I change. As we walk, the blurriness of *bigger* begins to come into focus.

There's nothing like watching your child take her first few steps. Ella spent months holding on to the edge of the couch. She somehow figured out a way to move through the entire living room without ever having to let go of a piece of furniture. For awhile, she was content to stay in one room, but eventually she wanted the freedom of walking without assistance. It was amusing to watch her wrestle with letting go.

The first few times she let go and took a step she wobbled, lost her footing and fell over. But as she continued to step out, she eventually got the hang of balance. With each little step she learned how to stabilize her muscles and support herself. Before long she was walking, one step at a time, on her own.

Allowing God to rebuild leaves us wobbly at first. We don't see the *bigger* plan. Our balance comes as we let go and trust His hand to steady us.

chapter eight

Catching Your Breath

Nehemiah may have been in mourning over the brokenness back home, but he still had a job to do where he was. Life doesn't stop because things get difficult. Nehemiah's job as cupbearer to the king was very important. He would have been one of the most trusted men in all of Persia. As Nehemiah waited for God to move him, he also continued to work. I wish the world stopped when I stop. But we all know, hard things happen and life goes on, with or without us. How did Nehemiah go back to life while experiencing such heartbreak?

Nehemiah's calmness and strength, inspires me. I am so quick to take action. Nehemiah sensed God's call to go and rebuild the wall, but he never jumps the gun. He doesn't rush in declaring, "This is what God wants me to do!" Rather, he waits for God to move.

There is such wisdom in slowing down. Because of his job, if Nehemiah were going to do something about the wall, he could not do it without approval from the king. Getting permission was going to be hard. Timing would be everything. King Artaxerxes would have to empathize with the people of Jerusalem enough to grant Nehemiah the permission needed to go and rebuild the wall.

One particular afternoon as Nehemiah went before the king with his wine, the king noticed Nehemiah seemed burdened.

"The king said to me, 'Why do you appear to be depressed when you aren't sick? What can this be other than sadness of heart?'" (Neh. 2:2 NET.)

The king asked Nehemiah what seemed to be bothering him. Nehemiah told the king about the walls. What happened next is a discipline I pray will overtake my life.

"The king said to me, 'What is it you want?' Then I prayed to the God of heaven, and I answered the king" (Neh. 2:4–5).

I am jealous that Nehemiah's gut reaction when the king first asks him what he could do to help, was prayer.

"Then I quickly prayed to the God of heaven" (Neh. 2:4 NET).

He knew what the king could do. The king had resources and power that could make this journey much easier. Nehemiah, heartbroken, fearful, unsure what the future held, could have spit out a thousand words to the king in that moment and instead he silently whispered a breath prayer.

There was no time for a long, drawn-out prayer with all the right elements, but he had time to breathe and if he could breathe, then he could pray. Through prayer, he could release control and know God walked before him. There was no need for panic. God was already involved. He was already knee deep in the issue Nehemiah faced. A simple breath prayer would be enough. When we let God into what's broken and spend necessary time at His feet, we can be confident in the small prayers we pray throughout the day. He knows, He hears, He is well aware and ready to be involved.

BREATHING BIGGER

In the beginning, I wasn't sure what God wanted me to do with the word bigger, so I started praying, "Bigger." I had never done a breath prayer before, but in the case of Yosselin and her family, brokenness quickly brought me to the end of myself, making it a good time to start. *"Bigger"* became my breath prayer.

I disciplined myself to breath out anxiety, fear, sin, my temptation to control the situation, or the frustration of not knowing what to do next. Then, I inhaled His Spirit. I inhaled His power, His grace, and His wisdom. As I exhaled the second time, I whispered the words, *Be bigger, be bigger in this, be bigger in me, and be bigger through me. Be bigger, Jesus,* became what I prayed each morning as Ella closed the car door and ran into her school building. *Be bigger, Father. Be bigger in her. Be bigger through her. Be bigger in this place. Bigger in her teachers. Bigger in her friends. Bigger in her future."*

It was my answer when things felt overwhelming during the build, *Be bigger Father. Be bigger in this house. Be bigger in this family. Be bigger in this project. Be bigger than this cancer.*

The breath prayer is powerful because it doesn't come from our mind, like most of our prayers. Rather, it comes from the depths of our desires and our need to access more of Him. It is so simple it does not require a lot of thought to remember, yet it is so deeply attached to our heart it has the power to transform our mind in mere seconds. It spills out of our mouths, at times before we even realize it, as we relinquish control to him. It becomes what you do, who you are, and where you go to access God's presence at a moment's notice.

Breath prayers don't replace our other prayers, rather they support them. They enable us to pray without ceasing and walk in step with the Spirit. They open up opportunity for inviting Him into every situation. They refocus and reenergize us, as we walk toward *bigger*. The breath prayer gave me a connection with the Spirit of God in a powerful way. Praying no longer stopped when I left my secret place each morning; rather, praying went with me, all day long. I carried an awareness of His presence everywhere I went. Everything looks different as you walk in step with the Creator of the universe.

There were days I whispered, *"Be bigger,"* without even realizing it. His word took over my thoughts and before I knew it I was depending on Him to be *bigger* in everything. My breath prayers didn't change Him. He stayed the same. My breath prayers changed me. I was developing a new level of intimacy with the Spirit living inside of me. God had more access to my life than I had ever given Him before.

What I realized was, I didn't merely have the Spirit of God living in me so I could do big things for Him; I had the Spirit of God living in me so He could do big things in me. He wanted to grow me. He wanted to pull me in to this intimate place where His voice was louder than the voice of this world. As God became bigger in me, what He could now do through me became *bigger* as well.

RUACH

"'My grace is sufficient for you, for my power is made perfect in weakness.' Therefore I will boast all the more gladly about my weaknesses, so that Christ's power may rest on me. That is why, for Christ's sake, I delight in weaknesses, in insults, in hardships, in persecutions, in difficulties. For when I am weak, then I am strong. (2 Cor. 12:9–10)

The more intimate time I spend with Jesus, the weaker I become. The good news is the weaker I become, the stronger He becomes. If I do not become weak, He does not get the opportunity to be strong. For years I have worked toward being strong in my faith, all the while thinking the end goal was to achieve a level of spiritual growth putting me at the top. When the truth is, He wants me at the bottom. He wants me dependent. It is only through dependency that I gain access to the places He longs to take me. His power is made perfect in my weakness. It is not in my strength that I will experience more of Him.

When the walls come down, we do anything to connect with Him, but sometimes, as the initial blow subsides and the pieces of our lives come back together, our temptation becomes to rely on our newfound strength. With a little less desperation in our voices and a little less trembling in our legs, we are sometimes tempted to start walking independently. As the moments of intense prayer and fasting decrease, the temptations to depend on oneself increase. It doesn't take brokenness for us to depend on God, but when brokenness presents us with the opportunity to depend on Him, we need not be tempted to take the reins back at the first sign of stability.

Most times we do it without even noticing. The framing of Yosselin's house was up and the roof being put on. We pulled into the dusty driveway that morning overwhelmed at the task before us. We had come on a mission. We had come to pray, to give back to God what was rightfully His, this project.

"MAYBE WE'LL JUST"

We must have looked crazy as we stepped onto the worksite with our workout clothes on and to-go coffee mugs in hand. I laugh when I think about what the roofers must have said, but we were desperate.

Just the night before Angie and I met for coffee and to discuss details about furnishing the inside of the house. Our conversation took a turn as we realized the expense of the task in front of us. Before we knew it we were saying things like, "Maybe we just do carpet and not hardwood. Maybe we only furnish the main living area and use their old furniture for the bedrooms. Maybe we don't purchase the new dishes and we leave that for them. Maybe we just this, maybe we just that."

At the same time, we both realized what we were doing. Our strength gets us into "maybe just," conversations like the above. Our strength does not get us to bigger. *Bigger* was not carpet, where Yosselin would only be able to access part of the house on her walker. *Bigger* was not putting their flood-damaged furniture back into a brand new, sparkling, shining home. *Bigger* doesn't cut corners. *Bigger* is abundance, it's more than we ever asked or imagined possible.

As Angie and I walked through the house that morning we laid hands on the walls and prayed, *"Be bigger, Jesus."* We laid hands on the windows and pleaded, *"Be bigger, Jesus."* We laid hands on the bedroom doors, the unfinished floors, the partial kitchen counters, *"Be bigger, Jesus. Please, be bigger, Jesus."* This was not about what we could do; it was about what He could do. It was about what He had started and what He would finish.

MY BREATH FOR HIS STRENGTH

The Hebrew word for Spirit is *ruach*. It literally means breath, air, strength, wind, and courage. As we breathe His Spirit, His *Ruach*, into our moments, we open ourselves up to His power. With *Ruach* in our lungs the struggle to keep our head above water ends. It ends because the struggle ends. Underwater is right where we need to be, fully submerged in His power.

Ezekiel 37:1–14 paints an amazing picture of how consuming the Ruach of God truly is. Each time we read the word breath in this passage, we are reading about the Spirit of the Living God (*Ruach*). This passage represents a vision illustrating the promises of new life that God gave His people. He promised them a nation restored, both physically and spiritually, regardless of its current condition. It's a lengthy passage, but so worth your time.

> "The hand of the LORD was on me, and He brought me out by the Spirit of the LORD and set me in the middle of the valley; it was full of bones. He led me back and forth among them, and I saw a great many bones on the floor of the valley, bones that were very dry. He asked me, "Son of man, can these bones live?"
>
> I said, "Sovereign LORD, you alone know."
>
> Then he said to me, "Prophesy to these bones and say to them, 'Dry bones; hear the word of the LORD! This is what the Sovereign LORD says to these bones: I will make breath enter you, and you will come to life. I will attach tendons to you and make flesh come upon you and cover you with

skin; I will put breath in you, and you will come to life. Then you will know that I am the LORD.'"

So I prophesied as I was commanded. And as I was prophesying, there was a noise, a rattling sound, and the bones came together, bone to bone. I looked, and the tendons and flesh appeared on them and skin covered them, but there was no breath in them.

Then he said to me, 'Prophesy to the breath; prophesy, son of man, and say to it, "this is what the Sovereign LORD says: Come, breath, from the four winds and breathe into these slain, that they may live." So I prophesied as he commanded me, and breath entered them; they came to life and stood up on their feet—a vast army.

Then he said to me: "Son of man, these bones are the people of Israel. They say, 'Our bones are dried up and our hope is gone; we are cut off.' Therefore prophesy and say to them: 'This is what the Sovereign Lord says: My people, I am going to open your graves and bring you up from them; I will bring you back to the land of Israel. Then you, my people, will know that I am the LORD, when I open your graves and bring you up from them. I will put my Spirit in you and you will live, and I will settle you in your own land. Then you will know that I the LORD have spoken, and I have done it, declares the LORD." (Ezek. 37:1-14)

Ruach was what brought the bones to life. *Ruach* gave them breath and stood them to their feet. *Ruach* rebuilt them into a vast army of God. *Ruach* is what I want bringing me to life. *Ruach* is what I want standing me on my feet and marching me out of brokenness. I may be out of breath, but the breath I have, His breath, is the only breath I need. *Ruach* never runs out.

I am no longer interested in doing this without His Spirit. Why would I settle for my own strength when His strength is one breath away? I want to breathe in the Spirit who makes me the army of God, because no matter how strong I become I will always be weak when compared to His greatness. I used to live for strength, but now I choose weakness. My weakness is strength when empowered by His *ruach*.

The same power that brought those dry bones to life is available to you. You are not expected to walk forward on your own. Inviting God into our dead and broken places brings the hope of new life. Giving Him *bigger* access lines us up with His *bigger* promises.

Prayer is our way of giving Him admittance. It is our way of inviting Him into the situations we face. Prayer is our connection to ruach. Powerful things happen inside of us as we pray.

"But when you pray, go into your room, close the door and pray to your Father, who is unseen. Then your Father, who sees what is done in secret, will reward you" (Matt. 6:6).

RESPONSIBLE DEPENDENCY

Breath prayers are about responsible dependency. You have a responsibility to be dependent on God. It is your responsibility to call out to Him during intense moments. The most responsible decision you will make is to line yourself up with the Spirit of God and allow Him to move in you whenever, wherever, and however He wants.

In the beginning we were scared to open our hearts to Yosselin, her family, and their brokenness. We couldn't see the *bigger*. On the other side we have no regrets. Instead of fear, we found faith. Calling on God for bigger impacted and shaped the people we have become. Today, I am thankful we could not fix the brokenness in the lives of the Randall family that cold afternoon in January. I am even more thankful we heard God's voice in the mist of heartbreak and invited Him.

Little did we know how our prayers throughout that year would change us. My desperate prayers changed everything inside of me and they changed everything outside of me. I am different, not because of anything I did, but because of everything He did. You want change? Do you want your life to look different, your brokenness to have purpose?

Start praying. Prayer never stops changing things because it continually lines our hearts up to the heart of God. Stop trying to catch your own breath while keeping yourself above the water and instead submerge yourself under the water allowing the ruach of God to take over.

What could be your breath prayer? *Bigger* worked for me. It allowed Him a *bigger* access to my heart, a *bigger* access to my marriage, a *bigger* access to my kids, to my family, to my faith, and to my future. I inherited so much from what the Spirit did inside of me with this little word that I would give it to you in a minute, but what if God wants to give you your own word? What if there is something God wants to do in you, transforming the very thing threatening to take you under?

I wonder what happens if you go after it? If you do what it takes to get your brokenness before the One who can do something with it. What happens if you look up, away from what's broken and let your eyes find Him in the mess? God is there; He is calling out to you, reaching His hands down and waiting to give you breath. He clearly sees what you are up against and has the strength necessary to move you forward.

"Even when I walk through the darkest valley, I will not be afraid, for you are close beside me. Your rod and your staff protect and comfort me" (Ps. 23:4 NLT).

Won't you call out to Him? Have your moment, weep, wail, and mourn, then in your mourning, call out to Him. Don't stop until you find Him and when you find Him, surrender the need to breathe on your own and invite Him to breathe for you. Rest in the assurance of the strength He promises. *Bigger* is your destiny. *Bigger* is your future. He will get you there because He has promised to, and we serve a God faithful to fulfill that which He has promised.

chapter nine

Turning Around

I blamed it on my friends. I blamed it on my family. I blamed it on the pressure. If you asked me while I struggled with the broken, it would have been anybody's fault but my own. It's always easier to let others be responsible. My girls' first instinct is to point the finger at one another. Taking ownership is rough.

My first two years of college were spent in a cycle of defeat. I desperately wanted out of the brokenness in my life, but no matter what I did, it gripped me. I could not gain the momentum necessary to move forward. It was as though I continually lifted my foot to take a step, but then never reconnected with the ground below. I was stuck and for years I blamed it on everything other than myself. I claimed to hate the mess I was in, yet I stayed.

WHAT ARE YOU FACING?

I sometimes overthink repentance. I hear the word *repent* and think of dramatic, scenes with sackcloth, ashes, weeping, and runny mascara. And although it's healthy to experience intense moments of emotional repentance and sorrow over the sin keeping us from God's perfect plan, we also must grow in our ability to simply admit we're going the wrong direction, turn around, and follow God.

In its most simple form, repentance means acknowledging God isn't facing the same direction we are, and then turning around. Repentance is best represented in a change of direction. "We repent when our sorrow over sin leads us to the place where we receive power from God to change the way we think." [3]

After Nehemiah spent time weeping and praying over the brokenness represented in the destroyed walls of Jerusalem, he then physically changed his direction. He stopped facing the kingdom of Persia and turned to face God's Kingdom. He recognized God behind him and adjusted himself accordingly.

Turning around is a critical step as we journey toward *bigger*. *Bigger* is always the opposite direction of broken and it is impossible to follow God with our backs toward Him. We follow what we face. Nehemiah's prayers connected him to God, but then he had to move. After finding God in the broken, we must be willing to turn and face Him.

God is always at work. He is always there; pray until you find Him. Once you find Him, turn around and face Him. He has something in mind for you. Something He wants to do in you and something He wants to do through you. He will find you as you weep. He will answer you when you cry, but once He does, it is up to you to follow Him out. True repentance happens when we turn from what we face and follow Christ.

I overstayed my time in brokenness because my repentance was based fully on my emotions. I wanted to move more than anything. As a young adult I despised who I had become. I was tired of being who everyone else wanted me to be. The idea of being consumed with a love for Jesus sounded so inviting. I wanted the life He intended me to have, but was stuck in the life I had created. No matter how much I cried or how hard I begged, I stayed exactly where I was.

The problem wasn't what I wanted. The problem was what I faced. What I faced was what I served. As long as I stayed facing my sin, I was unable to follow God into *bigger*. He wasn't interested in my feeble attempts to rebuild what had been broken. He had a plan, a perfect plan in fact, but it required turning around. He loves it when we cry out to Him, but when we find Him, He expects us to turn around and follow. Nehemiah heard God's voice in his brokenness, he got up, brushed himself off, and followed.

SIDE HUGS

Have you ever been in one of those uncomfortable "side-hug" situations? Being at different churches gives me a lot of opportunity to interact with people. Some of them I can't wait to hug, the embrace and love are right on and much needed! But then there's always those awkward, crooked side hugs that never go as planned.

I find that sometimes I come out of brokenness offering Jesus a crooked side hug. My response to Him is hesitant. Though I recognize the sin, I still face it. Though I see the deception, I don't deny it. I understand the need for forgiveness, but I am still hesitant to turn around and fully embrace it. In my unwillingness to follow through, I remain facing the brokenness and therefore remain consumed by it.

Jesus doesn't do side hugs. He's the all-or-nothing type. No part of Him wants you to repent only enough to be forgiven. He wants your full, complete, totally open, ready for life change, repentance. He is looking for a complete embrace. It is with your back completely turned on sin and brokenness, that He will lead you to *bigger*.

The Ark of the Covenant was a big deal in the Old Testament. It represented the physical presence of God. Without it God's presence was not with His people and they were lost. In 1 Samuel, God's people lost possession of the Ark while battling the Philistine army. The Philistines took the Ark of God and set it up in their temple. For seven months the Ark stayed there.

While the Ark was in Philistine possession the Philistine people were plagued with disease and sickness. Each morning the Philistine leaders walked into the temple to find their god, Dagon, lying facedown before the Ark of the Covenant. Unwilling to test the God of the Israelites any longer, the Philistines packed the Ark up nicely and sent it back where it belonged.

When the Ark arrived at the camp of the Israelites, Eleazor took possession of it. "During that time all Israel mourned because it seemed the LORD had abandoned them" (1 Sam. 7:2 NLT).

For twenty years, the Ark had been back in the Israelite camp. God's people had been crying out to Him in despair for years. Feeling abandoned and forgotten about, they mourned over the loss of God's presence.

Wait! What? God's presence was back, the Ark was in their possession. It had been for the past twenty years. God hadn't abandoned them. He was there. They were facing the wrong way. As they turned their faces toward their false idols, they turned their backs toward God. The Israelites couldn't see him because they were serving what they were facing. God's presence dwelled on top of the hill in Keith Jeriam, but at the bottom of the hill, God's people mourned.

Samuel comes onto the scene because God heard the Israelites in their cries. I am thankful for the Samuels in my life, those able to recognize when I am facing the wrong direction. Samuel came into camp and redirected their attention. "Listen, God is here. If you want to experience Him fully stop worshiping the idols standing before you. Turn around and worship God" (1 Sam. 7:3, author's paraphrase.). God hadn't forsaken them. They had their backs to Him. For twenty years, they faced their brokenness, crying out for *bigger*, when all the while it was one turn away.

Bigger existed for the Israelites; they simply needed to turn around. God's best is never for His people to live in fear and oppression; we were created to live in freedom. If you want to find *bigger*, find God, then do whatever it takes to turn and face Him.

LONELY NIGHTS

Here's where I got confused. I wanted to know God in my heart, but I never decided to do something about it with my feet. To determine something means to firmly decide. When you make your mind up in a determining way, you are no longer making an emotional decision. Determining is done with purpose and intent. Emotional decisions based on our hearts and feelings quickly lead us astray. Sitting down in our brokenness allows us the necessary time to process the overwhelming emotions surrounding us. Sitting gives time to recognize where God is standing and how we can best turn toward him.

On those lonely nights in college I cried out to God. *Make me love You. Please make me love You. I want to love You more than I love sin. I know there is more. Please show me.* Over and over again I repeated those phrases. I promise you, I meant every word of it. My heart really wanted to love Him more than the distractions in my life. But with my identity wrapped up in what I faced, I couldn't follow. Facing my sin kept my mind focused on the broken instead of the *bigger*.

With my back to God, I failed to recognize His ability to piece my life back together. With my back turned, I questioned where He was and if He would respond. I lacked the intimacy necessary to trust that He would walk me out of the broken and into the *bigger*. Facing what's broken prohibits us from seeing all God intends to do. Turning toward Him, we begin to catch glimpses of *bigger* and the life we were created to live.

I relate closely to the Israelites. God's presence was near, but I was too busy mourning the lack of connection I felt to notice. I needed more than a feeling.

Searching for help in turning, I signed up to go on a mission trip to Mexico. Surely working with orphans all summer would provide me the momentum I searched for. Something had to help me turn around. Have you ever put your expectation in an outside source to help you follow Jesus? That's completely what I was doing. In my head I decided this trip would be what I needed. It would give me the strength to surrender. It would convince me to let go of who I was and face Him.

Had I only known then what I know now! During those intense cries in my dorm room, God's heart was completely connected. He was already so in love with me and He longed for me to turn from the brokenness. He desperately wanted me to face Him. So much, in fact, that He would give me everything I needed to accomplish the task. I didn't have to seek an outside source to help me turn around. I only needed to seek Him.

He can't wait to embrace us and lead us through the process to *bigger*. We can trust His promises are good and true. Even in the deepest heartache, the most thoughtless sin, and the loneliest of all circumstances. He sees what we can't. He doesn't look at us and see who we are; He looks at us and sees who we can become.

Three days before the trip, I was in a life-threatening car accident. Driving back into town after a week with my best friend, I stopped my car at a red light. I remember the red light specifically, because it made me change my mind. Instead of sitting through the light, I turned right on red and made my way down Central Avenue.

I was taking a summer class and had an exam that morning. My goal was to make it to class with enough time to reread all my notes once more. It was at the next intersection everything changed. I don't remember the actual accident. I know I stopped at another red light. I even remember stopping. Witnesses say as I waited at the light, my car began to inch forward, making its way into the intersection and oncoming traffic. About the time my car reached the middle of the intersection a semi traveling the opposite direction swept me under the front of its back tires. Attached to the back tires of the semi, I was then dragged down the street. At some point, instead of crushing me, the car unattached itself from under the semi and was spit out into a brick wall.

Minutes later medics arrived on the scene and cut my lifeless body out of the car. The ambulance raced to a nearby field where a care-flight helicopter waited to transport me to the nearest trauma hospital. I don't know all the details of what went down in that helicopter, but I know the God I struggled to face quickly went to work on my behalf.

He showed up big for me that day. He rescued me from much more than a car accident. I woke up in the hospital a few hours later with my friends and family hovering over my bed, praising Jesus for my life. Outside of a few stitches and a major concussion, nothing was wrong. Not a bone broken, not even a scratch on my face. I still have the pictures of my mangled car in my desk. I don't want to ever forget all He did for me that day.

I was thankful to be alive, but still struggling to recognize the *bigger* in all the broken. Here I was stuck in bed when I should have been in Mexico. I didn't get it. If God was going to sweep in and save the day, why not intervene before the accident ever happened so I could still go on the trip I desperately needed?

Sitting in my pain and frustration, feeling sorry for myself and angry with God, I heard Him whisper to my heart for the first time, *I need you to know you can trust Me.*

I encountered Jesus that day in a way I will never forget. As I cried out, He answered me and for the first time I heard Him for myself. Hearing Him personally brought so much clarity. I was facing the wrong direction. *I* was the problem. It was me! It had been me all along. I was sorry over the sin in my life, but not sorry enough to turn my back on it. God's intentions were to move me to *bigger*, but I was facing the wrong direction.

During the days following my accident, I found the strength needed to turn around. As I did, He began to teach me about *bigger*. It wasn't about Mexico at all. I didn't need an outside source to physically turn me around. I simply needed to recognize God's heart. What I was looking for had been within me all along.

"The Lord is not slow in keeping his promise, as some understand slowness. Instead he is patient with you, not wanting anyone to perish, but everyone to come to repentance" (2 Pet. 3:9). I am thankful we serve a patient God. One who is willing to wait for us. One who fully understands *bigger* deserves our full attention.

DO YOU WANT TO BE WELL?

As Jesus traveled through Jerusalem to attend a Jewish festival, he encountered a paralyzed man in need of healing. It was normal for people with a disability— the blind, lame, and paralyzed—to lie near the pool because it was believed that when the water was stirred the first one to enter the pool would receive the healing they desperately desired. This man, in particular, had spent thirty-eight years alongside the pool hoping to be the first one in.

Jesus saw the man there, sitting in brokenness. Looking deeply into his eyes, He asked him, "Do you want to get well?" (John 5:6). Without even hesitating, the man responded with an excuse. "Sir, . . . I have no one to help me into the pool when the water is stirred. While I am trying to get in, someone else goes down ahead of me" (John 5:7).

Jesus looked intently at him and said, "Get up! Pick up your mat and walk" (John 5:8). At once the man was healed. He no longer needed someone to help him into the pool; he was standing before the ultimate healer. The healing he searched for didn't come from the cool water below him; it came from encountering the Jesus in front of him. Jesus was in town, which meant he had everything he needed to be healed right there!

Jesus changed the crippled man's perspective. He showed him the truth behind the healing he sought. It wasn't about what was broken, it was about who was fixing it. The most effective thing we can do in brokenness, is stop looking at the broken, stop analyzing the resources in front of us and simply make eye contact with the One who longs to restore us.

Without repentance, we stay locked in place. What if I told you Jesus stands behind you, waiting? What if what you have been looking for is one turn away? Jesus comes asking, "Do you want to be made well?" Our answer lies in our movements. We answer with what we do. Jesus isn't looking for a, "Yes, but." He is looking for a change in direction.

"Their loyalty is divided between God and the world, and they are unstable in everything they do" (Jas. 1:8 NLT).

Ouch! No way do I ever want to come across as divided between the things of this world and the things of God. My loyalty lies with God, but so often, with my inability to turn to Him when dealing with the brokenness, my loyalty becomes divided.

Early the other morning I texted my friend Dana, *I'm not sure what's going on, but I feel heavy inside. Will you please pray for me this afternoon while we are together?*

A few hours later we sat together in a meeting. Once the meeting ended and the room cleared, I confessed what I thought the problem was, "I feel like God has asked me to take every thought captive. I cannot allow the enemy to run rampant with what's going through my mind about the future and things I cannot control."

"That sounds right," she said. "Tell me how you are doing that."

"I'm noticing the direction of my thinking and putting a stop to the thoughts that are not uplifting," I answered her. "But it's not going away, the heaviness; it's still there," I said, with big tears running down my cheeks.

She put her hand on my leg, "I wonder if you are supposed to do a little more than just stop the thoughts." She kept talking but my mind immediately went somewhere else. That was it! That was exactly what I needed to hear. God was trying to get my attention. He asked me to receive healing concerning my thoughts. I turned, but I hadn't turned all the way. I was the crippled man sitting by the pool recognizing healing was available, yet not actively embracing it.

STRONG WILLED DETERMINATION

Ella's determination to do things herself wears me out, but our heavenly Father has an unlimited supply of patience. He is not worn out by our strong will. He stands right behind us, arms out, extending healing. If you aren't sure, take a minute and notice Him. Try it with me, stand or sit still, really still. Take a deep breath. Breathe in and breathe out slowly. Do you feel Him? Is He there, right behind you, arms out, extending healing?

"He heals the brokenhearted and binds up their wounds" (Ps. 147:3).

Those first few weeks after my accident, I felt the hand of my Savior reach down and bind up my pain. This time, instead of stubbornly declaring I could carry it myself, I let go and turned around to follow. With Him holding the weight of my hurt I found the strength I needed to face the *bigger* I didn't fully understand. Turning my back on the brokenness allowed me to fully embrace His redeeming plan for my life.

Nehemiah surrendered his future too. He surrendered his will, threw his hands in the air and shouted out to God, "Whatever it costs, repair the damage. I sense You in what's broken. I sense You in the brokenness of your people. Use me as You restore hope. Show me what to do, show me where to go, show me how to do it."

As Nehemiah turned his back on the life he knew and faced the living God, things began to take on a new perspective. God always waits to embrace us fully on the other side of repentance. He anticipates the moments when we allow Him the privilege of binding up our pain and walking us toward *bigger*. It's what He lives for; it's what He died for.

Turn around.

Notice Him.

Embrace Him.

Recognize the *bigger*.

chapter ten

Battling the Mind

There is wisdom in letting brokenness force you to the ground to cry it out, because on the other side of strong tears we tend to think more clearly. Following Jesus out of the broken is an intentional choice.

The human mind thinks anywhere from twelve thousand to fifty thousand thoughts per day. The majority of these thoughts are based on our social environment and geared toward our own preference. Allowing emotions from our many thoughts too much control will quickly leave us circling the drain in doubt and fear.

"Finally, be strong in the Lord and in his mighty power. Put on the full armor of God, so that you can take your stand against the devil's schemes. For our struggle is not against flesh and blood, but against the rulers, against the authorities, against the powers of this dark world and against the spiritual forces of evil in the heavenly realms" (Eph. 6:10–12).

More times than not, I think fighting a physical battle would be easier than the spiritual battles we fight every day. Nothing feels better than a long run after a hard day. Being able to run out frustration and sweat out failure is so healthy.

Unfortunately the battle we fight is much different. Spiritual battles don't play by the same rules. We battle an unseen enemy over control of very real emotions. Our enemy fights to oppress and distract us. With each step, our attention to the *bigger* leaves him fuming in defeat. He will use any means possible to keep us from reaching our fullest potential in Christ. Because of their sheer power to control our actions, our minds are often the first place of attack.

The enemy is a liar. Therefore, we must train ourselves to recognize when his deceiving ways are before us. "When he lies, it is consistent with his character; for he is a liar and the father of lies" (John 8:44 NLT).

RECOGNIZE THE LIES
KNOW THE TRUTH

In order to recognize the lies, we must first know the Truth. Bankers are taught to identify counterfeit bills by memorizing what the real bills look like. They study the weight, appearance, and smell of the actual bill, because a counterfeit bill may come across the counter in many forms. Learning to recognize all the disguises of the enemy would be impossible. He has many tactics and presents himself in many forms. The most effective way to arm oneself against his schemes is learning to recognize the Truth.

"The weapons we fight with are not the weapons of the world. On the contrary, they have divine power to demolish strongholds. We demolish arguments and every pretension that sets itself up against the knowledge of God, and we take captive every thought to make it obedient to Christ" (2 Cor. 10:4–5).

Have you ever found yourself in the middle of an argument and realized you don't know all the facts leading up to the disagreement? It is hard to discern when to stand strong and when to fold when you are not equipped with the full knowledge of truth. The Word of God is the only weapon enabling us to demolish strongholds, arguments, and false accusations. The Word is the only weapon with the ability to overcome doubt, fear, and anxiety. The Word will destroy selfishness, envy, and pain.

"The word of God is alive and active. Sharper than any double-edged sword, it penetrates even to dividing soul and spirit, joints and marrow; it judges the thoughts and attitudes of the heart" (Heb. 4:12).

I recognize the enemy in my anxious thoughts. When God's peace seems far off and worry threatens to overcome me, I realize I have allowed his voice to muffle the voice of my Father. We do not serve a God of anxiety. We serve a God of peace. Our identity is in Him, not in the things we do or the things we can't control. Our future is in His hands and with that promise comes all the peace we need.

Knowing the Word is necessary to recognize how the enemy pursues you. What are the lies you fall victim to? Where do you feel inadequate? Where do you feel condemned? Abandoned? Alone? Rejected? Helpless? Hopeless? If God is the giver of all good things, then rest assured these feelings are not from Him. We cannot embrace the *bigger* while falling for the lies of the enemy.

KNOW THE SPIRIT

Sometimes things don't sit right. We may not even know why, but we feel it inside. Something's off. My first reaction is to push away the gut checks as nothing, but I have an active Spirit living inside of me worth taking notice of.

From the moment we hand our lives over to Jesus, we receive His Spirit. The Spirit is always there and always working. We sometimes don't recognize Him, but rest assured He's there. The more intimate we become with the Spirit of God living inside of us, the more we begin to recognize the movements of

God outside of us. The more we begin to recognize the movements of God, the more what is not of God will stand out.

It is impossible to fight an enemy we don't recognize. Knowing
God's Word is critical. We cannot afford to entertain anything
contradicting what the Word says. Nothing gets control over us
without our approval. Even in the midst of extenuating circumstances, we have the ability to control where our minds go. We
must train ourselves to know the Word and to know the Spirit,
so we are better equipped to distinguish Truth from untruth.

Cultivating a relationship of intimacy with the Spirit is much
like beginning a friendship with another person.

"You are My friends if you do whatever I command you. No
longer do I call you servants, for a servant does not know what
his master is doing; but I have called you friends, for all things
that I heard from My Father I have made known to you" (John
15:14–15, NKJV.)

If He wanted to, God could tell us what to do without giving us
other options. But instead, He invites us into a relationship. He
provides us the eyes, ears, and mind of Christ so we may learn to
tune ourselves in to what He is doing. He extends an invitation.

Even the best friendships take work. They take sacrifice, surrender, a heart to listen, and a willingness to respond to the needs
of the other person. Over time trust is developed. My closest
friends have the freedom to say whatever they want about my
life because I trust the intentions of their hearts are for me and
not against me. God created us to be in relationship with Him.
His Spirit inside of us longs to build a life of intimacy where

trust runs deep. This relationship will be what enables us to recognize Him quickly.

REFUSE THE LIES

Recognizing the lies is not enough. After recognizing untruth we must then refuse to allow it to take root in our lives. There are times I have been quick to recognize the lies of the enemy, but slow to do anything about it. During these times I walk in oppression, allowing the heaviness of defeat to control my thoughts and actions.

Learning to recognize the lies is what gives us opportunity to refuse them. We recognize them, then we hand them back. We turn our ear away, shake them off, run them out—whatever it takes to get rid of them.

It helps me to think of it like this: we have the privilege of refusing the lies the enemy speaks over our lives. It is my privilege not to partner him. I have been empowered to tell him no. I get to push him off and there is nothing he can do about it. We do not miss out on *bigger* because the enemy slips a thought of deception into our minds here or there, rather we miss out on *bigger* when the unrecognized deception takes root and grows into something more.

In one way or another, we eventually have to deal with the prisons the enemy builds in our minds. How many times have you allowed a thought to turn into more? How many times has a simple word spoken out of context turned into a massive offense? How many times does hurt turn into bitterness? The initial thought was not the issue. The issue came by not recognizing and refusing all that followed the thought. As lies collect, the enemy builds. Brick by brick he works, leaving us captive to the control of something other than God. In our negligence the seed sown takes root and begins to grow into what it was never meant to be.

We don't know what thoughts ran through Nehemiah's head as he processed the broken state of God's people. But he must not have allowed his mind to dwell on lies such as, *They brought this on themselves; if only they had followed the Lord instead of idols; they need to learn their lesson. Or even doubts like, I can't rebuild an entire wall; my job as cup-bearer is too important; the king will never approve this ridiculous request, I might as well not ask.*

Nehemiah battled both inside and out to embrace the *bigger* plan God put in front of him. The enemy recognizes when *bigger* is on the horizon and he steps it up. He, no doubt, went after Nehemiah with his A game during Nehemiah's intense moments of prayer and repentance. He feared once Nehemiah embraced the *bigger* God was putting in front of him, it would be hard to change his mind. Nehemiah pushed through and recognized Truth from deception. He turned his back on the enemy and determined in his mind to follow God to *bigger*.

"Commit everything you do to the LORD. Trust him, and he will help you" (Ps. 37:5, NLT).

The enemy only advances as far as we allow him, because he holds no power over us and has to flee the minute we refuse him.

"Resist the devil, and he will flee from you." (Jas. 4:7).

What does resisting the devil look like? It looks like us telling him no. It looks like refusing to take in his lies, even for a minute. It looks like training our minds to filter truth from untruth and having the courage to toss the untruth out with the garbage, the minute it rears its ugly head (or beautiful in some cases). It looks like getting a little righteously angry when he thinks he can sneak one in while you aren't looking. That's not his place. We don't belong to him. We have the power of the Almighty God living within us, the authority to take every thought captive and make it obedient to Christ. It is our privilege to refuse.

REPLACE THE LIES

Replacing is important. If you go to the gym, you might notice the serious body builders chugging a white, powdery mix after they finish a workout. What they are doing is important to the muscles they are building. The nutrients in the powder quickly mix with the muscles, providing strength and vitality. All the extra nutrients increase the rate of growth and development.

I once had a friend who drove her car until she blew the engine. The oil light was on and she never did anything about it. Stopping week after week to fill up with gas wasn't helping. A car will only run for so long with the light on. Refilling the oil is important.

Knowing the majority of our thoughts consist of the things we allow access to in our lives, warrants us to pay better attention to our surroundings. Sometimes getting to *bigger* requires a willingness to lay aside mind-numbing distractions. We cannot expect to recognize and refuse the lies of the enemy successfully for long if we continually replace what we spit out with more lies.

We speak things into being. Meaning, what we say eventually becomes what we do. What we do eventually becomes who we are. Dave is an amazing dad, but what would happen if I told him every day how terrible a dad he was? What if I pointed out every little thing he did wrong and continually drew his attention to the misses he had with our girls?

I can predict what would happen. Eventually, he would start to believe the lie. Even more so, as he started to believe this lie, he would inevitably begin to act it out. He might start second-guessing how much our girls love him. He would likely start doubting the way he disciplines them, holding back for fear of doing it wrong. He would probably withhold affection, thinking he is doing them a favor by not getting close to them. Before you know it, he would be distant and hurt, guarded and unavailable. All because of one lie. One lie can do extensive damage when allowed to take root.

The things we take in with our eyes and ears have to be processed somewhere. God's Word warns us to guard our minds because He fully recognizes what we don't. Growing up playing soccer, I knew training was not an option. We worked hard in and out of season, so we would be better prepared each time we stepped on the field.

Fight for your mind. His lies do not get to define you. They do not have power over the person you are becoming. Believing them will definitely keep you from *bigger*.

For years the enemy spoke the lie of shame over my life. I carried the burdens of my past on my shoulders instead of walking in the freedom Christ promised me. Shame sometimes kept me from praying for weeks. Not because I didn't want to pray, but because the enemy convinced me I didn't deserve to pray. I messed up too many times. God's grace was enough, but it wasn't enough for me, not this time, not again.

Brokenness sometimes leaves scars. The good news is, those scars are not your identity. You get to be a part of the *bigger*. You are promised freedom, forgiveness, and grace. You have the privilege of replacing the lies with the Truth. When you refuse the words of the enemy, he has to leave. When you replace his words with Truth, the Truth will take root, enabling you to stand stronger than before.

If you find yourself having a hard time replacing the lies, try replacing some of the things surrounding you. Think about what you listen to, what you read, the conversations you have, the places you go; the things you take in have to be processed somewhere. What do you spend your time doing?

"If your right eye causes you to stumble, gouge it out and throw it away" (Matt. 5:29).

Jesus's words here are pretty extreme. I think He means, if that book makes it hard for you to be married to your husband, stop reading it; even better, throw it away so no one reads it. If that show makes you want what you cannot afford, turn it off. If that friend entices you to fall into sin you have sworn off limits, find a new friend.

As much as we wish the old saying to be true, things rarely go in one ear and out the other. Participating in the *bigger* purposes of God is a privilege. This privilege comes with great responsibility. God will continue to show up and blow your mind with what

He does in your life, if you will continue to be responsible with what he shows you.

If the promises of God are not winning out in your life, start by looking into your mind. It's possible the battle started long before you realized it. Change the way you think and it will change the way you act. Be protective of the things you take in. Take in things leading you to *bigger*. Soak yourself in thoughts that create a hunger for more of God. Turn your ear toward words that leave you with a holy expectancy of the *bigger* things He is capable of.

chapter eleven

Staying Surrendered

The journey from brokenness to *bigger* always involves a process. Staying surrendered to the process often proves to be the hardest part of the journey. Sometimes I avoid admitting brokenness, because I am resisting the process. However long and painful, the process is necessary because it creates the space God needs to work in us.

We are presented with multiple opportunities each day to join Him in *bigger*. *Bigger* is not about us. It is about God partnering with us to bring the Kingdom to earth. Submitting to the process is essential because God always intends to do a work in us before He will do a work through us. Surrendering to the process comes on the other side of recognizing what's broken and turning around. The process is all about shaking off the past, letting go of the future and allowing God to show you the new way.

No matter how long we are in process, the end always presents us with the ladder needed to climb to *bigger*. The process is the muscle-building leg of the journey. God intends to take us somewhere, but we must ready ourselves. Climbing before our legs are strong enough always ends badly.

The process is where transformation happens. It's where strength is gained, muscles are built, and perseverance is developed. The process enables our mind to better recognize the mind of Christ. It is often where we realize *bigger* isn't actually about us at all. It's about Him and His Kingdom.

Before the process we often think we are ready for *bigger*.

In the middle of the process, we are tempted to give up the *bigger*.

On the other side of the process we let go and celebrate the *bigger*.

GOD'S WORKING

Nehemiah turned and followed God into Jerusalem. He surrendered to the call of rebuilding the broken wall. The question now was *how*. God rarely lays out the details of the entire process ahead of time; rather, He gives us what we need to know one day at a time, increasing our faith and dependency on Him every step of the way. Nehemiah boldly stepped into the process. He surrendered his identity as cupbearer to the king and allowed God to go to work in his life.

When the Spirit begins to move in the midst of what's broken, you can rest assured God is at work. If you let Him have His way, He will do a work inside of you to better prepare you for *bigger*. Nehemiah loaded up, officers of the king's army in tow, and started his journey. He had what he needed to get him safely to Jerusalem, but upon arriving he had to go to God for more details.

> I went to Jerusalem, and after staying there three days I set out during the night with a few others. I had not told anyone what my God had put in my heart to do for Jerusalem. There were no mounts with me except the one I was riding on. By night I went out through the Valley Gate toward the Jackal Well and the Dung Gate, examining the walls of Jerusalem, which had been broken down, and its gates, which had been destroyed by fire. Then I moved on toward the Fountain Gate and the King's Pool, but there was not enough room for my mount to get through; so I went up

the valley by night, examining the wall. Finally, I turned back and reentered through the Valley Gate. The officials did not know where I had gone or what I was doing, because as yet I had said nothing to the Jews or the priests or nobles or officials or any others who would be doing the work" (Neh. 2:11-16).

Nehemiah arrived in Jerusalem in secret. He didn't come shouting about all God was going to do. That would be foolish, because he didn't know what God was going to do. God had called him out of mourning and led him to begin the journey toward *bigger*, but where to go from here was still in the works. God will get us to *bigger*, but He will not skip the process.

LAYING OUT THE PLAN

While everyone slept each night, Nehemiah snuck out to survey the land. He carefully inspected the damage done to each section of the wall, noting where the work needed to begin and what was necessary to see this project all the way through. *Bigger* was on the horizon, but there was much to do before the work began.

Spiritual transformation is the process by which Christ is formed more fully in us. It is the process of us becoming more like Him. Spiritual transformation allows one to gain new perspectives on what it means to live for God's glory. Surrendering to the process of transformation increases our capacity to discern and do the will of God. In order to survive in *bigger*, we must first undergo the process. The process is hard because it is not something we control. It is Him, working within us.

"God can do anything, you know—far more than you could ever imagine or guess or request in your wildest dreams! He does it not by pushing us around but by working within us, his Spirit deeply and gently within us"(Eph. 3:20 MSG)

METAMORPHOO AND TRANSFORMATION

Spiritual transformation is hard to understand because it is a paradox. On one hand it is natural for Christ followers to grow and change, but on the other hand it is supernatural, the way God uses the Holy Spirit to launch us into such change. Transformation is something you dedicate yourself completely to, but it is not something you can completely do.

"Do not conform to the pattern of this world, but be transformed by the renewing of your mind. Then you will be able to test and approve what God's will is—His good, pleasing and perfect will" (Rom. 12:2).

The Greek word *metamorphoo* refers to the process by which a caterpillar enters into the darkness of a cocoon in order to emerge a butterfly. I've never studied the mind of a caterpillar, but I highly doubt the caterpillar goes into the cocoon fully understanding the *bigger* waiting on the other side. Still, the caterpillar surrenders to the process of transformation, trusting the unknown lying between it and *bigger*. Likewise, our journey of transformation requires us to relinquish control and give ourselves over without a full understanding of what all will take place as God prepares us for *bigger*.

Ella was terrified to ride a bike without training wheels. As adults, we know riding a bike without training wheels is great.

No one puts training wheels back on once they have experienced bike-riding freedom. We worked diligently for weeks to persuade Ella to take the step. It was an agonizing task. She worked up the courage to get on the bike and get going, only to jump off of it into safety before we had the chance to let go.

It had to be done; she had to learn to ride her bike. You cannot be six and ride your bike to school with the training wheels still on. In order for this to work, I needed Ella to trust me. She had to trust I knew what I was talking about. She had to believe it was in her best interest to learn to balance her bike on her own. She must trust my intentions. I would not let go until I felt her balance kick in and even when I let go I would be right there ready to help her up if she started to wobble.

When we turn to face the *bigger* things of God, we can't possibly see what He sees. Our minds simply aren't ready yet. We are limited to seeing who we are and the things right in front of us. The Father sees the *bigger* on the other side of us. Trust and surrender will keep you committed to the process, even when it gets difficult. God always has our best interest in mind. Giving up after a few skinned knees would be like putting the training wheels back on after the very first fall.

Building Yosselin's house transformed my mind. I saw God move in incredible ways. I learned what it meant to walk in His power and operate in His authority. During the project our pursuit of *bigger* changed the way I looked at myself, the way I looked at God, and even the way I looked at the world. I had access to Him in ways I never thought possible

Throughout the build, whatever we asked for, God gave. If we needed workers, He provided. Money, He found it. Publicity, the phone rang. It was as if He were there, the sixth man on the team, the go to player, waiting to pull through with the game-winning shot at a moment's notice.

Looking back, I see how He was working even without our knowledge. He was behind the scenes intimately moving in the hearts and minds of the people we would need in the future. He was preparing the soil for what we couldn't see. And as if that weren't enough, the entire time He was working through us, He was also working in us, transforming our minds so we could fully grasp the reality of the Kingdom.

VINES AND BRANCHES

"Jesus said to them, 'My Father is always at his work to this very day, and I too am working'" (John 5:17).

Jesus sat with his disciples and painted a detailed picture for them of what spiritual transformation looked like. It was important they understood the process they had been in and the fruit that would soon grow due to their surrender.

"I am the true vine, and my Father is the gardener. He cuts off every branch in me that bears no fruit, while every branch that does bear fruit he prunes so that it will be even more fruitful. You are already clean because of the word I have spoken to you. Remain in me, as I also remain in you. No branch can bear fruit by itself; it must remain in the vine. Neither can you bear fruit unless you remain in me" (John 15:1-4).

The gardener goes to work in his vineyard with the main goal of producing the most abundant grapes possible. As he walks up and down the rows, he looks first for the branches producing no fruit at all.

The fruitless branches are usually low to the ground, covered in dust from the road. With the rain, the dust would quickly be turned to mud, weighing them down. The increased weight leaves them barely exposed to the sun, if at all. Even attached to the vine it is not possible for such a branch to produce fruit. Fruit requires exposure to the sun.

John 15 says after noticing such branches the gardener will "cut off" every branch not bearing fruit. The Greek word Jesus uses here is *airo* and is correctly translated "lifts up." In other words, God will lift up every branch that doesn't bear fruit.

This creates a very healthy image. It is not God's desire to rip things out of our lives, point a finger at us, and lecture us about what we can and cannot have. Rather, He desires to pick up what has been pushed into darkness, clean it off, and expose it to the light, in hopes of bringing the dead to life.

The gardener doesn't stop after the barren branches either. Once he has lifted up the fruitless branches, he will then walk through the vineyard a second time. This time, he walks through with the intention of pruning the fruitful branches. He prunes fruitful branches in hopes of producing even *bigger* fruit. Success comes when he yields a more abundant crop than the year before. God's intentions are always for us to have *bigger* fruit.

Bigger fruit is a product of trust and surrender. We must trust the gardener and his intentions for us. As he works his way through the garden, pruning our lives, our only job is to stay surrendered.

As the Israelites neared the Promised Land, abundance was so close you could taste it. God told Moses to send twelve spies ahead of them to observe the people currently inhabiting the land. The spies quietly approached their destination. Once there, they cut down a branch with a single cluster of grapes so heavy it took two of them to carry it back. A cluster of grapes so large it had to be draped over a pole and carried between the shoulders of two soldiers.

Today we are happy to go to the store and buy four clusters of grapes in one small bag. When God told His people He had a land flowing with milk and honey for them, He wasn't exaggerating. A life of *bigger* is a life of abundance. It's more than we could ever ask or imagine. It's out of our grasp, away from our doing, and something produced by the hands of the master rebuilder.

Before experiencing *bigger*, I settled comfortably in the land of big. They weren't the best grapes, but they were enough. I could live with them. Or so I tried to convince myself. No matter what I did, I knew there was more. There had to be more. Building Yosselin's house increased my appetite for *bigger*. Experiencing more of God left me wanting even more. Our team tasted what it was like to walk in His abundance and we couldn't get enough of it. As the project came to a close, I was so hungry for more I literally begged God to walk through the vineyard of my life.

Bigger fruit was mine for the taking, but it would come only on the other side of trust and surrender. God will do the impossible through me, but first He will do the impossible in me. There was a process and I didn't get to skip it.

IN THE TENT

Joshua was Moses's assistant. Whenever Moses met with God, Joshua went with him.

"Inside the Tent of Meeting, the LORD would speak to Moses face to face, as one speaks to a friend. Afterward Moses would return to the camp, but the young man who assisted him, Joshua son of Nun, would remain behind in the Tent of Meeting" (Exod. 33:11 NLT).

Moses left the tent to go back and deliver God's message, but Joshua stayed in the posture of abiding. Instead of running to join Moses, he soaked up the presence of God as long as he could. Joshua knew *bigger* was for him, but it wasn't for him right now. He was a work in progress, committed to staying at the feet of his Master, until he was ready for the challenges ahead.

There are seasons in life when it is best for us to remain in the tent. As we sit with Him, He does some of His best work. Abundant fruit comes from resting in His presence. When we work, we work. When we sit with Him, He works. In the process we begin to recognize the *bigger* on the horizon, but arriving there prematurely will leave us unprepared.

PREP TIME

What if what the enemy meant for bad, God meant for good? The walls around Jerusalem were down, leaving God's people sitting in brokenness. In brokenness, they had time to look up and notice they were facing the wrong direction. If the walls didn't get rebuilt quickly, the enemy would control their future.

Who would have guessed being set free from captivity would have actually been a death sentence?

The broken walls and cries of God's people allowed Nehemiah time to notice which direction he was facing. In his cries, he found God. Nehemiah felt compelled to repent and change direction as he surrendered to the unknown waiting for him. He found the momentum needed to turn his back on life as the king's cupbearer and partner with God as they journeyed toward *bigger*.

Inside the transformation process we are checked, challenged, and changed. There are many things we only learn in surrender. "Between the promise and the payoff there's always a process. That process is where your audacious faith comes into play. Without the process, there is no progress. But the process is usually filled with pain. And if you don't know how to process the process, you probably won't make it to your promised land. That's why audacious faith is so vital. It brings your unseen future possibilities into focus right now. It redirects your attention from what is right now to what you believe will one day be." [4]

The process is full of pruning. It is full of exposure, it's full of letting go, but surrendering to the process is what brings *bigger* into focus. The more patient we are, the deeper we allow Him to work, the more brokenness He will reveal. The more brokenness He reveals, the more healing we receive.

"Are you tired? Worn out? Burned out on religion? Come to me. Get away with me and you'll recover your life. I'll show you how to take a real rest. Walk with me and work with me—watch how I do it. Learn the unforced rhythms of grace. I won't lay anything heavy or ill-fitting on you. Keep company with me and you'll learn to live freely and lightly" (Matt. 11:28–30, MSG).

THE SECRET PLACE

He has a call for us, He has plans to partner with us in *bigger* ways, but the first place He calls us is to himself. Oswald Chambers wrote, "When God gets us alone through suffering, heartbreak, temptation, disappointment, sickness, or by thwarted desires, a broken friendship, or a new friendship—when he gets us absolutely alone, and we are totally speechless, unable to ask even one question, then He begins to teach us." [5]

In your secret place, Jesus goes to work on your life to develop the faith needed for the climb to *bigger*. Jesus works best in the secret place because there is no hiding. In the secret place, we allow God to shine light into our lives and reveal truth. As He weaves His way in and out of the vineyards of our heart, we see the reality of barren, fruitless branches and with surrender we are given new opportunity to hope.

Looking back at my life I recognize many times when God awakened me to *bigger*; they are times full of much abiding and much surrender. They were times where I spent more hours of my day with Jesus and aware of His presence, than I did without Him and unaware of His presence. I didn't find life-changing revelation in a crowded room with loud music and a passionate speaker—I may have found a spark in those moments, but the fire grew as I spent time together with Him, cultivating a relationship in my secret place.

I have a dark-red wooden desk in the corner of my family room. The desk sits right next to the large windows cascading down the back of our house. In the morning, as the sun shines, it warms my chair. This is the spot I meet with Jesus most regularly. It is my secret place, the place I spend the most intimate time with Him. It is in this place I am able to open myself up and pour out my true feelings. In this place I meet with Him. In this place I expect to hear from Him. In this place, He expects to hear from me.

The place is significant to me because the encounters taking place there change me. As I sit with him, I am checked. I am challenged and, mostly, I am changed. Sitting with Him, I wrestle through surrender and obedience, letting go of what I thought I wanted and embracing the plans He has for me.

"But when you pray, go into your room, close the door and pray to your Father, who is unseen. Then your Father, who sees what is done in secret, will reward you" (Matt. 6:6).

The secret place is not so much about location in a physical sense as it is about a spiritual place you get yourself to with God. It takes time for God to work through your brokenness. He needs time and space. We need time and space. Finding this is difficult and many times it is the one thing keeping us from *bigger*, but I have yet to look back and see that more time with Jesus was wasted time. We don't ever walk away from His presence disappointed and lacking.

Jesus was always in high demand. Everywhere He went, people followed. He had all the success and attention He needed, but over and over again He forsook the crowd to meet with the Father. "Very early in the morning, while it was still dark, Jesus got up, left the house and went off to a solitary place, where he prayed" (Mark 1:35).

Jesus's ministry was birthed out of the secret relationship He had with His Father. He didn't need the acceptance of the crowd. His identity wasn't in what they thought of Him. Jesus walked in obedience with authority and power, because of the connection he had with his Father. Meeting with the Father, in the secret place, strengthened the covenant relationship they had. Jesus came to provide a way for us. It is through His sacrifice we find life. His death was not an easy task. It was from the strength of the Father, He was able to accomplish the task before Him. It was from that strength, he was able to humbly obey, even when it meant death.

"'No eye has seen, no ear has heard, and no mind has imagined what God has prepared for those who love him.' But it was to us that God revealed these things by his Spirit. For his Spirit searches out everything and shows us God's deep secrets" (1 Cor. 2:9–10, NLT).

On the other side of repentance, God has a *bigger* plan for us, but first He must build the muscle, enabling us to get there.

Having a secret place with God requires deliberately shutting the door on everything else and opening the deepest parts of oneself up to Him. In the secret place we develop a love for Jesus simply because of who He is and not because of what He can do. The secret place represents us seeking after the presence of God, more than the promises of God.

More than anything, God desires to connect with us intimately. There is a connection available to you in the secret place with

Jesus that you cannot get anywhere else. The deeper I get into my secret place, the more I fall in love with Jesus. As we work to cultivate our friendship, He lets me in on things I wouldn't otherwise know.

"I no longer call you servants, because a servant does not know his master's business. Instead, I have called you friends, for everything that I learned from my Father I have made known to you. You did not choose me, but I chose you and appointed you so that you might go and bear fruit—fruit that will last—and so that whatever you ask in my name the Father will give you" (John 15:15–16).

The secret place is where a foundation of friendship with Jesus is established. *Bigger* quickly fades when it isn't birthed out of this all-consuming, passionate relationship. Knowing what God is doing comes from knowing God's heart. In the secret place, we become friends with Jesus. In the secret place it stops being about where we are going and starts becoming about with whom we are going.

"If anyone wants to become my follower, he must deny himself, take up his cross, and follow me. For whoever wants to save his life will lose it, but whoever loses his life for my sake will find it" (Matt.16:24–25, NET).

God is calling you to *bigger*, but getting there will cost you your life. You cannot step on your ladder and start climbing with your own life on your back. As you sit next to Jesus, in your secret place, you will be able to discern the difference between His life and yours.

COUNTING THE COST

A few years ago we took a group of students to Monterrey, Mexico, for a Back2Back mission trip. Before leaving home, Dave and I had been deep in conversation about the cost our girls paid as we surrendered to a life of full-time ministry. Working in the church world meant our weekends very much belonged to ministry. With the girls in school now, we were noticing the cost. Weekends looked different, sports looked different, what we could and could not be a part of was beginning to look different. I found myself wondering if our girls were missing out because of God's call for our family.

Each day in Monterrey, God drew my attention to the Back-2Back staff kids on campus. I noticed how they interacted with the guests, how quickly they were drawn into worship each night and how eager they seemed to be a part of the *bigger* mission going on. Our last morning there I realized there was not a staff kid there who thought they were "missing out."

They lived life on mission. They live life in *bigger* and it didn't appear to bother them. The cost was worth the gain. Giving up our lives may sound harsh until we fully encounter Jesus. Upon fully encountering Jesus, nothing is too much.

"The kingdom of heaven is like treasure hidden in a field. When a man found it, he hid it again, and then in his joy went and sold all he had and bought that field" (Matt. 13:44).

The man knew the importance of the treasure he found. The treasure was worth everything. As we grow closer to Jesus in our secret place, the length of time we fight surrender decreases. If you find yourself counting the cost, go deeper. Fall even more in love with Him and see if surrender doesn't come easier.

My time spent abiding with Jesus in the secret place led to the surrender of things I didn't even know were standing in His way. I had to make space. I had to look harder. I had to dig deeper. *Bigger* was on the horizon, but there were things in His way.

In my secret place, I found the strength to offer up my pride. I surrendered my need for the approval and acceptance of the people I serve. I surrendered my fear of failure and laid down control of my future. I let go of my identity and embraced Him.

Typing this now, on the other side of extreme surrender, it seems far too simple. Surrender is a battle. It's is always a battle. Paul doesn't tell us to die to ourselves because it is easy, but *bigger* is worth it. Surrender will cost you, it will cost you everything. But, you never regret *bigger*.

In his secret place, Nehemiah was able to connect with God and see His heart for the *bigger*.

> I went to Jerusalem, and after staying there three days I set out during the night with a few others. I had not told anyone what my God had put in my heart to do for Jerusalem. There were no mounts with me except the one I was riding on. By night I went out through the Valley Gate toward the Jackal Well and the Dung Gate, examining the walls of Jerusalem, which had been broken down, and its gates, which had been destroyed by fire. Then I moved on toward the Fountain Gate and the King's Pool, but there was not enough room for my mount to get through; so I went up the valley by night, examining the wall. Finally, I turned

back and reentered through the Valley Gate. The officials did not know where I had gone or what I was doing, because as yet I had said nothing to the Jews or the priests or nobles or officials or any others who would be doing the work." (Neh. 2:11–16)

Nehemiah shows such wisdom by not running ahead and jumping on his ladder. God purposed his heart to rebuild the wall, but Nehemiah surrendered to the process. He got out of the comfortable to better see the movement of God. Climbing to *bigger* was going to take work. Hard work, which needed to be fueled by the spiritual muscles he would develop in the secret place.

NEVER GIVE UP

There will come a point in the process when quitting seems easier than pushing forward, when the hill seems too steep to climb and *bigger* too far away. Whatever you do, don't quit. Go deeper. It's worth it. *Bigger* comes on the other side of broken, but you have to keep moving. Don't opt out because you're tired; don't opt out because you think you have given enough. Stick with the process. The most painful tension often comes right before the most life-changing victories.

Nehemiah pressed through and on the other side he stepped on his ladder and began the climb to *bigger*. The Nehemiah who climbed onto his ladder was a different Nehemiah than the one sitting in brokenness weeping, wailing, and mourning months earlier. He knew God differently and he knew himself differently. He had been transformed.

What is the bigger you need to climb to? Where do you need more of Him than you could ever imagine? Where do you need rest and repair? Where is it you have lost hope? On the other side of brokenness you get a bigger, but you have to surrender to the process before you get there.

chapter twelve

Stepping on My Ladder

Stepping onto your ladder signifies it's time to work. God has done a work in you and now he wants to do a work through you. As we climb, He partners with us to bring His message of redemption and rebuild His Kingdom.

Knowing God differently enabled me to impact my community differently. As He changed me, He also invited me to partner with Him and help change those around me. *Bigger* wasn't only for me. It was for my family. It was for my friends. It was for my community. It was for everyone I encountered.

In July, almost seven months after we met Yosselin, we bulldozed her dilapidated old home. Now the work could begin. Up to this point our hardest work was done in the secret place, in our prayer closets, as we begged God to be *bigger*. God had been working all along. He rallied the community, gave us a voice and increased our faith enough to believe in the impossibility of His promised *bigger*. We were positioned for the climb, ready to go to work.

Climbing onto our ladder gives us the chance to impact the world we live in.

NEHEMIAH'S LADDER

The evidence pointing to how Nehemiah changed came when he stepped onto his ladder and started working. On the other side of the process, we are given the opportunity to point others toward the transforming power of encountering Jesus's healing process.

Turning from brokenness and sitting at the feet of Jesus awakens something inside of us. Time with Him opens our eyes to things we have never before noticed. No matter how long it takes, abiding always presents us with internal growth and an external opportunity for more.

Nehemiah repented before God, he surrendered to the process, walked away from the life he knew, and embraced a life in God's Kingdom. Changing directions put him in Jerusalem, secretly making plans to rebuild what was broken. On the other side of the process, Nehemiah now had the faith necessary to step onto his ladder and do the work God purposed him to do.

Rebuilding is never easy. Climbing to *bigger* after brokenness is one of the hardest things you will ever do, but it is completely possible. You have developed the muscle mass needed to bear the weight. In five months I will run a half marathon. Last week, I started training. You could say I have stepped onto my ladder. There is a place I need to go, or really a distance I need to run— 13.1 miles. In order to get there I am going to have to work hard. I am going to have to make a plan and I will most definitely have to be accountable. Climbing this ladder will be difficult. It's cold, and I hate running outside in the cold. The only thing worse than running outside in the cold is running inside on the treadmill. There will be days I don't want to run, days I don't have time to run, and days I physically can't run. On those days I have to train myself to remember the race, remember the plan, and remember my partner. Success comes from remembering why I started in the first place.

Stepping onto our ladders gives us direct access to *bigger*. On the ladder we show the fruit of our newly transformed mind. During our climb to *bigger* the enemy works diligently to knock us down. We are most dangerous to him here and he knows it.

The enemy came after Nehemiah. Trouble rose for him from all angles, but Nehemiah remembered God. He remembered the *bigger* he was called to carry out and he remembered his people working alongside him. The ability to remember enabled Nehemiah to press through and withstand the enemy's attacks.

God intends for *bigger* to come from what is broken in our lives and He is willing to do a lot of work to get us there. Up to this point we have done a lot of seeking, sitting, praying, and preparing. Our ladder represents work. The desire for *bigger*, without the discipline to get there, doesn't amount to much. Rebuilding happens because God does what is necessary in us, and then we do what is necessary to move forward.

Nehemiah took many steps in preparation; now it was time to step up.

CLIMBING TOWARD BIGGER

The climb to *bigger* represents growth. God always has more in store than where we currently find ourselves. There is always a *bigger* for our lives, for our marriages, for our families, for our friendships, for our future, or our faith. Wherever you currently are, there is *bigger* on the other side.

Nehemiah had a job to do. There was now a new purpose at foot. He was climbing his ladder, putting the wall back together, encouraging the work of God's people, and defending the nation of Israel. On the other side of brokenness, we too find purpose. Like Nehemiah, with a new purpose in our hearts, we are presented with the opportunity to climb.

For some of us the climb will be the hardest part yet, but *bigger* is within reach and this new reality changes our mindset. It is imperative we step onto our ladders committed to remember. When the enemy attacks, we remember God and the work He has done in us, we remember the *bigger* and the new purpose He has connected our hearts to, and we remember our people, the ones we climb with as well as the ones we climb for.

Climbing up our ladder puts a target on our back for the enemy. We are now doing the work of the Kingdom in a more powerful way than ever before. We are actively partnering with God to rebuild the broken. We are the restorers. We are bringing freedom and healing to those around us. This is an issue for the enemy. He attacks with the sole purpose of bringing you down off your ladder.

As you climb, remember well.

REMEMBER GOD

Allowing God to be Lord over my life means I give Him full authority, full control, and full power to do what He wants, whenever He wants. It means I recognize I am no longer the author of my own story; He is and I have accepted His invitation to play a role in the *bigger* story He scripts.

Some of us will have an easier time remembering this than others. I have to remind myself of his authorship daily, because I prefer to be the main character. The more I remember God; the more I want to remember Him. Living for Him has brought satisfaction in ways I didn't realize were possible. Living for myself never felt this good. To live for God means to set aside the thing inside of us and go after a life totally free of self. It means to want what he wants.

I work hard to remind myself of who God is and what role I get to play in His story each day. It tends to go over best when I remember Him first thing in the morning, because, for me, it only takes a second for His Lordship to go out the window. If I handed you my prayer journals and you flipped through the pages you would see page after page of reminders. Over and over again, I have reminded God of whom who He is in my life—not because He needs to be reminded—but because I do!

One of my favorite things to do is to look back through my journals and see all the things God has become to me. I can tell exactly what I was struggling with by how my prayers remind God of His place in my life. It is great to watch the words of my prayers change from phrases like *Please be my comfort, please be my peace, please be my strength,* to *You are my comfort, You are my peace, You are my strength.* Those prayers changed me; they strengthen me and enable me to keep climbing.

Experts say it takes twenty-one days to create a habit. Something physically happens in your brain once you have repeated something twenty-one days in a row to make it instinctual. As I practice remembering God and inviting Him to be *bigger,* it eventually becomes what happens instinctually.

Jesus spent countless hours remembering His Father. One of the most powerful examples we see is in Matthew 26. He knew the time was quickly approaching for Him to die, and being fully human, He wrestled with His role in God's story. Read His prayer. "He fell with his face to the ground and prayed, 'My Father, if it is possible, may this cup be taken from me. Yet not as I will, but as you will" (Matt. 26:39).

Jesus was God, but in this moment He was just like you and me. He would feel every bit of pain surging through His body over the next few days.

Jesus remembered.

"Have the same mindset as Christ Jesus: Who, being in very nature God, did not consider equality with God something to be used to his own advantage; rather, he made himself nothing by taking the very nature of a servant, being made in human likeness. And being found in appearance as a man, he humbled himself by becoming obedient to death—even death on a cross!" (Phil. 2:5-8).

No doubt Jesus didn't want to die the horrible death He knew He was going to. In His weakness, He fell to His face and called out to His Father. He cried out all night until eventually He found His strength.

This passage doesn't say Jesus was born humble. It says *he made himself nothing.* It was a choice. Jesus remembered His Father, He remembered the *bigger* and He remembered the people He climbed for. Remembering gave Him the ability to push forward.

We all need a daily reminder: *not my will Father, but yours.* We need a daily surrender: *Not my kids Father, but yours; Not my marriage, not my future, not my finances, not my job, Father, but yours.*

Our lives are not ours to live; they are His to live through us. We are here for His glory. He created us with purpose and intention. We exist to be a part of Him—every day, every hour, every moment.

REMEMBER THE BIGGER

Part of remembering God enables us to also remember the *bigger*. The *bigger* never overwhelms God. Though it is almost always too much for us, it is never too much for Him.

God will never let you down; He will never let you be pushed past your limit, because He will always be there to provide the strength necessary to continue. Life is going to be hard, at times overwhelming. There will be days the cost seems too steep. Even on those days, His promises are true.

"Meanwhile, the moment we get tired in the waiting, God's Spirit is right alongside helping us along. If we don't know how or what to pray, it doesn't matter. He does our praying in and for us, making prayer out of our wordless sighs, our aching groans. He knows us far better than we know ourselves, knows our pregnant condition, and keeps us present before God. That's why we can be so sure that every detail in our lives of love for God is worked into something good" (Rom. 8:28-29 MSG).

You can climb to *bigger*. The battle has already been fought, the victory already won. Rest assured, whatever you are facing right now, God is at work. He is moving and focused on getting you there. He sees how this will benefit you. He recognizes the strength in the person on the other side of this journey. He recognizes the *bigger* faith, the *bigger* family, the *bigger* friendships, and the *bigger* futures. He is not the cause of the brokenness, but, if we allow Him, He will work through it to bring *bigger*.

More times than not, the brokenness around me doesn't make sense. Yosselin's cancer didn't make sense. It did not make sense that her grandpa was working countless hours to provide for his family, yet their house was falling down around them. It did not make sense that grandma and grandpa were fighting this battle on their own and it didn't make sense we had just been invited into their journey toward *bigger*.

My insecurity in what I couldn't understand didn't shake God. He knew what I didn't. He knew what He was doing in the midst of Yosselin's battle. He knew exactly where He was going. He fully recognized the *bigger* we couldn't see. He kept his eyes firmly locked on it, patiently allowing us the blessing of the journey.

Our eyes are easily distracted. Focusing on the rubble lying around us tempts us to retreat into survival mode. In survival mode, I am in control. In survival mode, I call the shots. Control doesn't get us to *bigger*. Trust does. It is in trust that we stop, remember God, and remember the *bigger*.

"'For my thoughts are not your thoughts, neither are your ways my ways,' declares the LORD. 'As the heavens are higher than the earth, so are my ways higher than yours ways and my thoughts than your thoughts'" (Isa. 55:8–9).

REMEMBER YOUR PEOPLE

Enlisting the help of others is vital. Brokenness often reveals truth. Truth sometimes brings shame. The enemy wins when he uses our shame to keep us hidden from others. When shame lingers, remember God, remember *bigger*, and remember your people. By allowing fear to keep us hidden, we risk missing out on *bigger*. Nothing good grows in the dark. Our brokenness isn't news for everyone, but it is news for someone. We were not meant to do this alone.

Victory comes easier when we partner with people committed to the climb. It would do me little good to have a running partner who hates to run. We need to link arms with people willing to speak into our lives in a challenging way. We need people willing to pray for us, pray with us, and pray over us. We need people willing to recognize *bigger* on our behalf.

It is a valuable gift to find people who care more about God's bigger for our lives than our happiness and comfort. There is wisdom in searching to find the ones willing to battle for our faith, shed tears over our broken relationships, and push us to new heights.

The Apostle Paul was struggling. He surrendered to God's lordship, but the constant conflict he faced was overwhelming. As He remembered, God stepped in and provided for him through His people, "When we arrived in Macedonia, there was no rest for us. We faced conflict from every direction, with battles on the outside and fear on the inside. But God, who encourages those who are discouraged, encouraged us by the arrival of Titus. His presence was a joy, but so was the news he brought of the encouragement he received from you. When he told us how much you long to see me, and how sorry you are for what happened, and how loyal you are to me, I was filled with joy!" (2 Cor. 7:5–7).

Paul was trying to stay on his ladder. He recognized God had *bigger* things in store, but the opposition felt overwhelming as he climbed. God could have spoken directly to Paul. He had done it before. Instead, He sent Titus. Titus was exactly the motivation Paul needed to keep climbing. He was the encouragement, he was the strength, he was the person also climbing and willing to reach out to steady Paul's ladder when necessary.

We need others. My story is your story because our stories together make up part of God's story. We have the pleasure of doing this together. It is from your secret place with God that you learn to recognize His voice as He leads you to *bigger*, but He doesn't expect you to climb alone. We are better together.

If you are an introvert, finding other people may seem overwhelming. I have known people who never reach *bigger* due to the mere fact that they were unwilling to link arms with anyone to climb. I have stood confused as the enemy brought them down off their ladder time and time again, all because they had no one reaching out to steady them.

Freedom comes when you speak the truth out loud to the right person. One of the best things we can do is partner with someone climbing ahead of us. There is something to be said about living life. Wisdom, knowledge, and discernment grow as we go through the storms life throws our way.

I have Dana. She's in my life to help me discern what God is saying to me. She encourages me to listen and holds me accountable to respond. She speaks the truth in love and pushes me past my breaking point, so I may experience more of who He is in me. She says hard things, really hard things, but all with the heart to move me closer to God. She believes in me and encourages me to trust Him with the impossible. There are many things I have accomplished simply because she took time to steady my ladder as I climbed.

Then there's Crystal. She's in my life to remind me of who I am. She knows my entire journey, perhaps better than anyone. She was there when I had nothing left. She has a keen ability to see past the roadblocks causing me to stumble. Her words have more power to them than anyone else's because she has been there longest. I trust her to fight for me and with me.

These two ladies are ahead of me in this journey. They are committed to helping as I struggle to climb to *bigger* in all realms of life. They know *bigger* enables me to be of better use for the Kingdom of God and they are willing to do whatever it takes to get me there.

While I have people in my life to steady my ladder I am also a hand reaching out to steady the ladders of those around me. I have spent most of my life with high school students. As they seek out God's plans for their lives I find I am often in a position to point them toward *bigger*. As they prepare for their future it is my job to steady their ladder and encourage their faith. With each timid step, I remind them who God is, I remind them of His promises, and I remind them of their faith.

I almost gave up on having friends my age, until the night I met Angie at the coffee shop. I was tired of being burned by people who only seemed to care about themselves in the long run. I craved a friendship revolving around more. I wanted someone who didn't only want to have fun, but wanted to chase recklessly after God's *bigger*.

Angie was in the same place. Broken friendships and missed expectations left both of us sitting in a pile of brokenness. Inside the coffee shop it only took a few minutes for our conversation to get real. I expressed how tired I was of the disappointing friendships.

At the time we had no idea what all God had in store for the two of us. That conversation led us to an intentional decision to step onto our ladders together. The brokenness in our lives presented us each with an opportunity for *bigger*. Standing by our cars before we left that night we made the decision, without fully understanding, to turn our backs on our past definition of friendship and surrender to the process of becoming *bigger* friends. We would pursue *bigger*, together.

I always say, "I'm thankful Angie didn't know me before she knew me." What I mean by this is, I am thankful God had already done a work in my heart to prepare me for our conversation that night. God purposed us to benefit from one another and ultimately to add flavor to His story. Our friendship isn't a friendship about finding happiness and enjoying one another's company, it is about glorifying God and allowing Him to be bigger both in and through us. The overflowing blessing is, as we try to live our lives bringing glory to God, we find happiness and joy. By linking arms, sharing our plans, and climbing our ladders together we find a *bigger*, more satisfying friendship than we ever imagined possible.

> Two are better than one, because they have a good return for their labor: If either of them falls down, one can help the other up. But pity anyone who falls and has no one to help them up. Also, if two lie down together, they will keep warm. But how can one keep warm alone? Though

one may be overpowered, two can defend themselves. A cord of three strands is not quickly broken" (Eccles. 4:9-12).

We don't climb the ladder in our own power. Climbing the ladder comes entirely from the strength we get as we connect ourselves to the Holy Spirit living within us. And, even though we are connected to Him, there will be times when having a person next to us or directly above us will make all the difference in the world. It is amazing what steadiness an outside hand brings to a wavering ladder.

Angie has been my steady hand for four years now. We ask hard questions on behalf of one another. We face brokenness together, process pain together, and allow God to stretch us in crazy ways. We have difficult conversations when they must be had and cry vulnerable tears without hesitation. But we also laugh harder than we ever dreamed and experience more joy than in years of past friendships. Our ability to endure whatever the world throws at us comes from the one thing tying us together.

I believe God confirmed His approval of our desire for *bigger* when He invited us into the Yosselin project. It was only a few months after the intentional conversation outside of the coffee shop that I met Yosselin's family. After hearing their story and walking away completely broken, Angie was the first person I called. I knew God was calling me to *bigger*, but the fear of the unknown kept me paralyzed. Angie reached out her hand and steadied me. She was the calm voice in the midst of the unknown ahead. She saw what I couldn't see in the moment because of the tears blurring my eyes. For the next year, we worked side-by-side on our ladders as we each climbed toward bigger on behalf of sweet Yosselin and her family.

Nehemiah found strength in numbers. Together, as God's people climbed on their ladders to do the work of God, *bigger* was accomplished. Nehemiah remembered God. He called out to Him time and time again. He checked in with Him and allowed Him to rule. He remembered the *bigger*. He did not allow himself to be overwhelmed by the brokenness standing in front of him. He remembered his people. He would have been foolish to climb this ladder alone. He empowered an entire nation of people to step on their ladders and rebuild alongside him.

chapter thirteen

Outclimbing the Enemy

God never leaves us hanging on for dear life, ladders swaying in the wind. His intentions are for us to climb. Never are we a greater threat to the enemy than when we step onto our ladders. He recognizes the danger of our arriving at the top. There is something so satisfying about overcoming.

It's like a good action movie. Intense drama drives people together. The plot thickens and as the movie heroes fight through obstacles and overcome hardship, they learn to trust and depend on each other. They are bonded together. Things look different from the top of the mountain. Things feel different too. Jesus is different, your relationship is different, your outlook different. This type of different is good for us, but not good for the enemy.

The minute Nehemiah stepped onto his ladder, the opposition noticed. Nehemiah reaching *bigger* meant challenges for his enemies. Arriving at *bigger* changed the way God's people were protected. This change would affect their future productivity. It would affect their future control. The trajectory of their lives would be different should Nehemiah really finish the wall.

Sanballat was governor of Samaria, the region just north of Jerusalem. He may even have had hopes of becoming governor of Judea as well, but with Nehemiah on the scene all of those plans were thwarted. When Sanballat heard what Nehemiah intended to do, he became angry and the chatter began.

THREAT #1

Nehemiah and the Israelites were not even a day into rebuilding when the opposition started coming on strong with talk of defeat. Climbing onto my ladder opens my mind up for an intense chatter battle with the enemy. Most of the chatter exists inside my head, in the self-defeating form of doubt and discouragement, but sometimes it comes from outside sources as well.

Nehemiah had chatter going on all around him.

"'What are those feeble Jews doing? Will they restore their wall? Will they offer sacrifices? Will they finish in a day? Can they bring the stones back to life from those heaps of rubble—burned as they are?' Tobias, the Ammonite, who was at his side, said, 'What they are building—even a fox climbing up on it would break down their wall of stones!" (Neh. 4:2–3).

If this was the chatter going on outside of Nehemiah, I can only imagine the chatter going on inside. Is this really what God wants me to do? Am I crazy? Why would they be having such a fit if this were what God wanted? What if I am wrong, what if I fail, what if . . . what if . . . what if?

Sanballat's chatter was meant to ridicule the Jews. He called them "feeble," which means "withered and miserable." Their task looked foolish and unattainable to the opposition. Sanballat and Tobiah, another known enemy of the Israelites, saw the *bigger* as a threat. With a wall, the Israelites could protect themselves. With a wall they would have infrastructure. With a wall the future looked brighter for the Israelites.

The world succeeds by wealth and power, but God's people succeed in poverty and weakness. Sanballat mocked that it would take more than worship to rebuild the walls of Jerusalem. He accused them of not knowing what they were starting and not having the resources necessary to properly rebuild. The enemy mocks us as we attempt to lay down our lives and follow God's *bigger* purpose. He weaves webs of doubt, defeat, fear, and anxiety. Anything he can do to convince us *bigger* is not worth the risk.

When chatter starts and our ladders shake, we remember God, remember *bigger* and remember our people. Nehemiah took a deep breath and responded, "Hear us, our God, for we are despised. Turn their insults back on their own heads. Give them over as plunder in a land of captivity. Do not cover up their guilt or blot out their sins from your sight, for they have thrown insults in the face of the builders" (Neh. 4:4–5).

Nehemiah prayed through and gave the chatter back to God. He and his people continued building. They worked with all their hearts and rebuilt the wall until it reached half its height. With their hearts set on *bigger*, they climbed their ladders refusing to lose faith or give up. They persevered through their work knowing if God had called them to this task, He would see it through to completion. Making sense to the opposition wasn't necessary for them to climb to *bigger*.

The things other people say may hurt, but we cannot allow the pain to take us off our ladders. If we spend time mulling over words of the enemy, we will give him a foothold from which he can further attack us.

THREAT #2

As if the defeating taunts of the enemy weren't enough for Nehemiah, now talks of war began to circulate. Sanballat gathered the support of the surrounding cities and while the Jews worked, they moved in. When such threats reached Nehemiah and his people, they prayed to God and posted guards with both tools and weapons around the walls day and night. "Those who carried materials did their work with one hand and held a weapon in the other, and each of the builders wore his sword at his side as he worked" (Neh. 4:17–18).

Nehemiah never stopped working. He simply adjusted. With threats of attacks on the rise, the Israelites loaded up, weapons in one hand, tools in the other. Now they were both prepared to work and prepared to fight. Retreating was not an option. "Take the helmet of salvation and the sword of the Spirit, which is the word of God. And pray in the Spirit on all occasions with all kinds of prayers and requests. With this in mind, be alert and always keep on praying for all the Lord's people" (Eph. 6:17–18).

When threats arise, remember God. Believe what He says in His Word is true. Recite His promises. Memorize them. Repeat them both day and night. Do whatever it takes, but do not forget the *bigger* waiting for us. Nehemiah didn't come down off of his ladder for the chatter, nor was he coming down for idle threats.

Sometimes we don't give the enemy enough credit. He will use whatever he can to distract us from completing the tasks God puts in front of us. I sit right now on the verge of a life-changing decision. Both options are good, either one will be fruitful for the Kingdom of God. Having options is great! But this last week the options have won. The enemy runs through my mind, his chatter robbing me of the peace I am promised. Instead of anticipation and excitement, I find myself crumbling in fear and pressure.

THREAT #3

If something on the outside doesn't deter us, the enemy goes after the things closest to our hearts. Pressure from within takes perceived threats to an entirely different level. It is one thing to keep climbing in spite of those on the outside. It is entirely different to keep climbing in spite of those on the inside. Sanballat knew if he could turn the Jews against one another in discouragement they would eventually defeat themselves. Israel would crumble from the inside out. If he couldn't take them out from his camp, then he would take them out from within their own camp.

Discouragement is one of the enemy's best weapons. Discouragement kept the Israelites out of the Promised Land for all those years. It kept them wandering in circles worried and fearful. Discouragement takes a focused mind and turns it into a distracted mind. Causing us to look at how much work we have left and lose heart. Taking our eyes off God and *bigger* while on our ladder leaves us in a dangerous place. We cannot risk losing our footing by the distraction of discouragement. "But when you ask, you must believe and not doubt, because the one who doubts is like a wave of the sea, blown and tossed by the wind. That person should not expect to receive anything from the Lord. Such a person is double-minded and unstable in all they do" (James 1:6-8).

Almost to the top, Nehemiah had no time to pay attention to discouragers arising within his camp. He continued climbing. Nehemiah remembered God, he remembered the *bigger*, and he remembered his people.

The enemy was relentless and because of the continual threat of attack Nehemiah was forced to address the issues. The Jews were

terrified. Ten times they came to Nehemiah while he was working, pleading with him to do something. Nehemiah was not
afraid of the threats, but he saw how terrified his people were
and so he took another step of defense by posting guards at the
vulnerable places on the wall. Nehemiah called entire families
to stand and be ready for war. They would not go down without
a fight. God had purposed them. He had chosen them. *Bigger*
awaited them. "The LORD frustrates the plans of the nations
and thwarts all their schemes. But the LORD's plans stand firm
forever; his intentions can never be shaken" (Ps. 33:10-11, NLT.)

Noticing Jerusalem was prepared for their attacks, the enemy
backed off. Nehemiah made sure the men assigned to work
worked, and the men assigned to stand guard, stood guard. The
work had to continue. He positioned a man with a trumpet next
to him, so he could alarm the people immediately, should the
need to fight present itself. And onward they climbed.

Three-fourths of the way to *bigger*, we begin to recognize how tired
we actually are. At this point the excitement of a new adventure
has worn off and we feel the energy draining from our tired bodies. With the intense work of moving forward becoming our new
normal and the adrenaline no longer rushing through our veins,
we begin noticing the pains of our hard work.

In exhaustion we might even be tempted to cease striving. Worse
yet, with tired bodies we risk settling in a land less abundant
than the one God intends to take us to.

Noticing all the mayhem around him, Nehemiah called together
a great assembly, during which he addressed God's people and
called them out for their behavior. God was doing a work among
them and their selfish acts were unacceptable. They were allow-

ing things outside the mission to distract them. Their eyes turned toward worldly profits and acceptance and away from *bigger*. If they weren't careful, they were going to miss everything they were working for.

After their rebuke, Nehemiah then made the priests, nobles, and officials take an oath to do whatever necessary to restore order in their city and finish the wall. Disgusted with having to take time from his work to address such leaders, Nehemiah shook off his robe, a symbolic Jewish act of condemnation, and went back to work. There is simply no room for selfishness in the *bigger*.

THE LAST PHASE

Bigger was on the horizon. You could smell it. The wall had been built and all the gaps filled in. The only thing left to do was set the doors in place. In one last attempt to keep the *bigger* from being completed, Sanballat sent his messenger to Nehemiah, "Come, let us meet together in one of the villages on the plain of Ono" (Neh. 6:2).

Our work is not over until it is over. We must work to the end, because the opposition fights to the end. In a final attempt to stop the gates from going in place the enemy tried luring Nehemiah into working together. As an ally, Sanballat could defeat Israel from the inside.

Read carefully Nehemiah's response, "I am carrying on a great project and cannot go down. Why should the work stop while I leave it and go down to you?" (Neh. 6:3).

Four times they sent Nehemiah an invitation and four times Nehemiah responded, "I am carrying on a great project and cannot go down" (Neh. 6:3). Finishing the work was Nehemiah's intention. Taking time away, for any reason, was simply not an option. He was on his ladder, climbing to *bigger*. Any other meeting would have to wait.

Nehemiah's statement leaves me wondering how many times I have been within arm's length of *bigger*, only to allow the final ploy of the enemy brings me off my ladder.

You have everything you need for the climb. Expect to hear from the enemy as you step onto your ladder. He will notice and the attacks will come. Climb anyway.

> When you go to war against your enemies and see horses and chariots and an army greater than yours, do not be afraid of them, because the LORD your God, who brought you up out of Egypt, will be with you. When you are about to go into battle, the priest shall come forward and address the army. He shall say: "Hear, Israel: Today you are going into battle against your enemies. Do not be fainthearted or afraid; do not panic or be terrified by them. For the LORD your God is the one who goes with you to fight for you against your enemies to give you victory.. (Deut. 20:1–4)

Bigger is yours for the taking. Don't be scared. Don't be afraid. Don't be distracted. Take a deep breath. Remember God and all He is capable of. Remember the bigger and all He promises. Remember your people, allow them to steady your ladder while it shakes. Then, take a step up and repeat again and again and again. As many times as you need.

Breathe deeply.
Remember God.
Remember the bigger.
Remember your people.
Take a step.
Breathe deeply.
Remember God. Remember the bigger.
Remember your people.
Take a step.

section four

LIVING OUT BIGGER

chapter fourteen

The Reality of Bigger

Welcome to *bigger*. Looking back at the journey, it's not hard to recognize the intimate way God has been working in you. Arriving here was quite the task. You've no doubt cried (probably countless times), wrestled with truth, fought the enemy of defeat and left behind a part of who you used to be. You are different, more different than you imagined possible. It's probable you know God more deeply than you did before. He has revealed Himself in ways you might not have known existed. There is a deeper love here, a more intense relationship.

We don't have to be here long to know we don't ever want to leave. *Bigger* is a place of freedom and transformation. It is here that we live immensely satisfied, yet still empowered to strive for more. We fit better here. We were created for here and it is obvious. Life outside of *bigger* seems dull, ordinary, unexciting. We don't miss the person we used to be.

Our focus is no longer on who we were, instead we focus on who we are becoming. With a newfound freedom to strive for the impossible, we push forward. During the journey we were a part of some pretty amazing things, weren't we? It's likely that arriving here has helped you begin to dream. Our faith has grown and our endurance increased. We can now walk forward with confidence, not because of us, but because of Him in us.

It is here we see the *bigger* picture. God always rebuilds brokenness into *bigger*, it's His promise. "All things work together for good for those who love God, who are called according to his purpose" (Rom. 8:28 NET). Never does this statement make more sense than when we have the privilege of partnering with God as He uses what was once broken to bring others into the Kingdom.

Because I spend countless hours with teenagers, I am often present in their struggle to recognize God's voice. I have the privilege of pushing them to respond to the things He asks. There is nothing like helping someone recognize how much God is for them. And even better, how much He is in favor of their dreams!

The other day Julie walked into my office. It didn't take long to realize it was serious. She nervously played with her fingernails as she sat in a black corner chair. "What's going on, Julie?" I asked.

She hesitated for a minute, then confessed, "It's just . . . ummm . . . I've been having a hard time connecting with God lately and I don't know what to do about it."

I pulled my chair up closer to hers. "Okay, let's start with the obvious. Could something be in the way? Are you making time to spend with Him daily? Has He told you to do something that you haven't done yet?"

"I think I know what it is," she said with tears in her eyes, "I've been offered this internship at a different church. It's perfect, but it's not what I had planned. I think He wants me to take it, but I'm having such a hard time saying yes because it means I won't be here anymore."

My heart ached for her. I know what it's like for God to invite you into something great, but accepting that invitation meant denying something else really great. I recognized she was wrestling God for the *bigger*. She heard Him speaking and now she struggled through surrender and obedience.

I would give anything to be where these students are with Jesus when I was their age. I wish I had known how powerful God is and how desperately He wanted to play the lead role in my future. I didn't and thus I spent my years as a teenager in complete brokenness. Through wrecked relationships and disappointing friendships, I struggled to keep my head above water. As the years went on, I dug myself deeper and deeper simply trying to fit in. I pursued *bigger* on my own behalf. I pursued *bigger* on behalf of others. I bought the lie that I was in charge of my future.

On the outside, everything appeared perfect. But on the inside I was a complete wreck. On the inside, I knew I wasn't who they thought I was. I knew there was a God, in heaven, who had *bigger* plans for me. I knew He was calling me to a life of obedience and surrender.

I was broken, because I didn't know who I was. I was broken because I had allowed everyone around me to tell me what to do.

The walls hiding who I really was eventually crumbled (they always do.) Allowing God to put the pieces back together created in me a deep love for transformation. God transformed my mind. He renewed my thinking. A deep change has taken place in my life to better equip me for the work of the Kingdom. The more God allows me to work on His behalf, the more redeemed the brokenness of my past becomes. I serve out of what was once broken. By helping others recognize their identities in Jesus, my brokenness has now become my ministry.

Broken pasts look different from the *bigger* perspective. I don't know that I would jump to the front of the line when asked if I wanted to walk through all of the late nights, bad choices, and destruction again. But maybe I would, simply to know Jesus the way I know Him now. Somehow, on the other side of broken-ness, He made sense of my failures. He didn't cause my broken-ness, but He worked in spite of it. He is the master restorer, taking old things and making them new, taking the useless and making it useful. I am amazed at how good He is at what He does. No one could love me the way He has loved me. No one could give to me what He has given me. What a gift it is to expe-rience such victory in a place representing such defeat.

On the other side of the process, how do you feel different? What can you thank Him for? How have His goodness and mercy changed your heart through this journey? What might He be asking you to do with what you have learned? Do you have a new sense of purpose, a new sense of identity?

Sometimes we get so caught up in the work, we forget to stop and celebrate. Now's when you celebrate! You have worked hard. God has worked hard. Fruit has been produced. *Bigger* fruit. Maybe make a list. A list stating the ways God revealed Himself to you throughout this journey. It is amazing how quickly we forget how far He has brought us. Write them down and make a habit of returning to them often.

The journey from brokenness to *bigger* is a journey that will stay with you forever. It is a journey represented in becoming more of who God created you to be. Here's the good news. It doesn't have to end here, but you've probably already figured that out by now. Getting to *bigger* in one area simply sets us up for the journey to *bigger* in other areas. *Bigger* enables us to appreciate the broken. Brokenness is hard, but brokenness always leads to *bigger* when God is involved. The process is difficult, but standing on this side of brokenness we clearly see the process is necessary.

Throughout this journey, God has done a *bigger* work inside of you than you ever asked or imagined possible. He has taken you places you never thought you could go and the best part is He longs to show you even more! What if you surrender to a lifetime of not fearing brokenness? What if you surrender to a lifetime of allowing God to be *bigger* to you than anything else you come up against? What if you surrender to a lifetime of a *bigger* faith, a *bigger fight*, and a *bigger future?*

I believe in you and I am so deeply proud of you. Thank you for journeying with me. Thank you for allowing me to be real with you. Part of writing this story has allowed God time to rebuild some major brokenness in my own life. The words of this book were crucial for my journey of transformation. Through these words, I heard His voice and felt His Spirit. I found the encouragement to take His hand and walk in the other direction.

Thank you for allowing me to share my journey with you. It wasn't always easy. If I'm honest, I think I threw away more chapters than I kept. Thank you for trusting Him in brokenness. Thank you for believing. Thank you for looking up, making eye contact, and allowing Him to walk you toward *bigger.*

The power of transformation is represented in our ability to know and see Him differently. Remember God, remember who He is and remember what He has done for you. Remember how He came to you when you called. Remember the day He picked up your pain and carried it out of brokenness. Remember the impossible work He did in you, while you sat in your secret place. Remember how He lifted you onto your ladder and allowed you to recognize the *bigger* for yourself.

Please don't ever forget about *bigger*. Don't let this moment go to waste. Bask in it. Enjoy His goodness. Indulge in His satisfaction. Embrace His freedom. May *bigger* become what you live for. May nothing satisfy you the way *bigger* does. May you always long for it, both for yourself and for others. May you see what God sees and speak powerfully over others in the ways God has spoken powerfully over you. Go after them. Help them to recognize the *bigger* they can't fully identify on their own.

Never forget, you were not created to make this journey alone— not ever. Your stuff isn't for everyone, but your stuff is for someone. Allow others to invest in your life. Give them access. Invite them in. In turn, don't forget to offer yourself. Invite and invest in others. Nourish your relationships; guard them with all your heart, soul, mind, and strength. Pray together, grow together, and change together. We are always better together.

The final section of this book represents my prayers for you. As God has become *bigger* in my life He has also become *bigger* in my faith, *bigger* in my fight, and *bigger* in my future. The way I live out these three things will forever be changed because of the impact bigger has had on me. Allow His Truth to penetrate deeply. The transformation is only beginning. Live *bigger* out loud for the entire world to see and enjoy every second of it!

chapter fifteen

Bigger in My Faith

Our faith matters to God. He not only cares that we have it, but He cares what we do with it. Faith directly affects our ability to continually move forward into *bigger*. In *bigger* we trust God more. We trust His heart and we trust His ability to work on behalf of our future.

In Matthew chapter 5, Jesus tells a parable about a businessman going on a long journey. This businessman called his servants to him and entrusted them to manage his wealth while he was away. To one servant he gave five bags of gold, to another, two and to another, one. The first servant took his five bags of gold, invested them, and earned five more. The second servant took his two bags of gold, invested them, and earned two more. But the third servant, the one who received only one bag, dug a hole in the ground and hid his master's money in the ground, for fear of losing it.

When the master returned from his trip, he summoned his servants and asked what they did with his money. The servant given five bags of gold, brought those five as well as the five new ones he earned and laid them before the master. The servant given two bags of gold, brought those two as well as two more bags he earned and laid them before the master. When the master got to the servant he entrusted with one bag of gold the servant replied, "I was afraid and went out and hid your gold in the ground. See, here is what belongs to you" (Matt. 25:25).

I don't want to live life with my faith buried in a field somewhere. Sometimes the questions running rampant in my head get the best of me: "What if it doesn't work? What if they laugh? What if I look foolish? What if I don't have the right words to say?"

Just like the master gave gold to his servants, God has given each of us a portion of faith. It is what we do with our portion that makes the difference. We cannot bury our faith in a field and expect it to grow. We cannot wrap it up, hide it in the closet, and expect it to work miracles. Hidden faith will not push us to *bigger*. Hidden faith keeps us right where we are.

John Wimber, founder of the Vineyard Church movement, always said, "Faith is spelled R-I-S-K." In other words, if we want our faith to grow, then we need to do something with it. Faith grows by stepping out. When we step out, we create space for God to step in. When God steps in, He does what we cannot do. Witnessing Him do the impossible grows our faith.

God is honored when you take the necessary steps to increase your faith. He is committed to helping it grow.

FAITH AND UNDERSTANDING

Building Yosselin's house increased my faith. We were up against something impossible to accomplish on our own. Having our backs against a wall created many an opportunity to step out. Each time we stepped out, He stepped in. Each time He stepped in, He blew our minds with what He did.

Pursuing a *bigger* faith is intimidating because of what you must do to get it. Smaller says, "First help me understand, then I will step out and follow." *Bigger* says, "Help me step out and follow, I know understanding will come." It feels great to recognize when God is revealing something, but simply recognizing how He is moving isn't enough. Instead we must get comfortable moving with Him. If we continually hear God, but do nothing with what He says, we will stay exactly where we are.

Revelation is meant to draw us closer. The closer we are, the better we hear. The better we hear, the easier we follow. There is a huge difference in my step if I *know* God has told me to do something versus knowing someone else has told me to do something.

The winning combination we look for is a life of faith lived by coming in and going out. It is in coming close to Him that we better hear and recognize what He says; it is in going out and risking that we are able to find the confidence to trust Him more. The closer I get to Him, the more eager I am to share Him with the rest of the world. Likewise, the more I share Him with the rest of the world, the more aware I am of my need to draw closer to Him. The two go hand in hand.

"When anyone hears the word about the kingdom and does not understand it, the evil one comes and snatches what was sown in his heart; this is the seed sown along the path" (Matt. 13:19 NET).

In the experience, understanding often comes. *Bigger* is about finding the courage to step into the experience, even when we don't completely understand. *Bigger* believes understanding will follow. Biblical understanding far surpasses our intellect. It comes in the real-life risk of doing.

We cannot ask God to increase our faith, then ignore Him when He shows up with opportunity. Opportunity to step out leads to growth. I asked Dave for two years to paint and remodel our laundry room. Laundry is a pain and Pinterest, for some reason, has convinced me it would be less painful if the room I did it in was more delightful. Each time I asked Dave, he said okay and then never did anything with it. He never took the first steps to actually begin the process.

Eventually I caught on to his entertaining game and called his bluff. He was just buying more time. If God interrupts our lives with an opportunity to step out and we ignore Him, for whatever reason, we cannot expect Him to show up with something different next time.

DIGGING DITCHES

There is a great story tucked away in the third chapter of 2 Kings. In this fascinating chapter, we find the three kings of Israel are joining forces to fight a war they knew they could win. As with much of life, things did not turn out the way they intended. Midway through their journey, they ran out of supplies. Without food and water the men and animals would never even make it to the battle, much less have the energy to fight. In panic, the kings turned to one of God's prophets, Elisha, for help.

Elisha came back to them with a less than normal solution. He told them to go and dig ditches in a nearby field . After they finished the ditches, God would then fill them with water to replenish the men and cattle. The kings found Elisha's solution to be rather odd, but they trusted in God's promises and therefore did as they were told.

This story is all about faith. Only God could bring the results they were hoping for. What if they spent countless hours and energy they already didn't have, to dig ditches for no reason? It was risky. Did they believe God would step in? Could they trust His Word through His prophet to be true? To them, it was worth the risk. The kings and their people dug the ditches and when they woke up in the morning their land was filled with water!

What's the scariest thing God could ask you to do? What are the excuses already beginning to run through your mind? We all have our list of justifications ready for when God comes knocking. Our fears and our excuses don't matter, because what God is asking us to do has little to do with us. "God's gift to us is ability; our gift to God is availability. He says to us, 'You go first. You be available and step out, and I will empower you in the moment.'" [6] It's about God's grace and His desire to reveal Himself to the world.

The good news is if our faith isn't about us, then our lack of faith doesn't disqualify us. We are easily distracted by our shortcomings and our sense of limitations. Our doubts don't scare God. He is *bigger* than our doubts. When I doubt, it is because I am focused on myself. Faith is about trusting in His ability to do whatever I ask Him to do. With just a mustard seed size faith, God can move a mountain. Mountains move because it's not about us, it's about Him. If we trust Him, He will do what we cannot.

God has asked me to dig a few ditches in my lifetime. Some of His requests I have ignored, resulting in missed opportunities to partner with Him in the Kingdom. But other times, I quickly pull out my shovel and start digging. It never fails: when I dig, He shows up in *bigger* ways.

Three years ago, my oldest daughter, Ella, was set to start first grade. She was ready, but I wasn't. I feared so many things. She would be in school all day. Obviously, she was my first, because I thought this was a huge problem at the time. What I really feared was not being in control. Handing her over to the school and to teachers I didn't know made me nervous. What if they didn't treat her with love? What if they didn't like her? Worse yet, what if they did like her? Especially the boys! I cried out to God in my fear and He made it clear to me that keeping her home was not what He wanted for our family. I heard what God was saying, but continued to move forward with my own plan. It was a noble sacrifice to make. Surely God would get on board. For weeks I wrestled with the lack of peace I felt in the pit of my stomach. I was afraid and I wanted His answer to be different.

Eventually, I surrendered and obeyed. As a sign of my obedience, Ella and I went school shopping and left all the supplies on the kitchen table for the last two weeks of summer.

I dug a ditch. I didn't know what would happen when Ella went to school, but God did. He knew and if He told me to send her, I could trust it was in her best interest to be there. I can trust He loves her, even more than I do. As I walked forward in obedience I relied on Him for the necessary strength.

God is much *bigger* than we give Him credit for. He is more capable of working out the details in our lives than we could ever fully know. Shortly after Ella started school I had a conversation with her teacher, Marilynn. I mentioned to her that Dave and I were Pastors at the Cincinnati Vineyard. Wouldn't you know, Marilynn has gone to the Vineyard for years. She loves the Vineyard and she loves Jesus.

Leaving the school and walking back to my car that afternoon, I had to laugh. Marilynn was my gift from God. He really did know what He was doing. Not only did He fill my ditch, He overflowed it. Blessing always follows obedience. The warm summer sun beat down on my shoulders in the parking lot and I made an agreement with God to trust Him more.

Two months later, we met Yosselin and God started us on this *bigger* journey. A small act of obedience sparked the very words you are reading. There's no way we could have known all that was in store for this journey. Obedience always leads to blessing.

Ella going to school wasn't about me, it wasn't about Ella, and it really wasn't even about Yosselin. It was all about God. God saw an opportunity to make His love known to our community and He offered me the chance to be a part of it. I could have said no. I could have kept her home; it was an honorable thing to do. But I would have missed it.

It's possible I miss opportunities to partner with God almost every single day. His invitations are everywhere. His miracles are waiting. His Spirit is alive. Stepping out gives God opportunity to step in.

YOUR RESPONSE MATTERS

Simon invited Jesus over for dinner. Jesus was in town and it seemed like the right thing to do. As they are reclining at the table a sinful woman bursts onto the scene.

Earlier in the day she had heard Jesus's message and something inside of her resonated deeply with the hope He offered. Overwhelmed by His grace, she shoved her way into Simon's house uninvited. Standing behind Him, she was overcome with emotion and before she knew it, tears were streaming down her face. Most men only talked to her because of what they wanted from her. Jesus was different. He offered to give her something. He didn't condemn her. He welcomed her.

Simon had invited Jesus into his house as a guest. Upon His arrival, Simon barely acknowledged Him. He was in the presence of royalty and remained unaffected. He did not greet Jesus with a kiss, he did not offer to clean His feet, nor did he anoint His head with sweet-smelling oil. All of which was customary when inviting a guest into your home during ancient times. Simon asked Jesus to show up and when Jesus showed up, he didn't even acknowledge His presence. Simon may have said yes to Jesus on the outside, but in all of his actions he was saying no.

This woman didn't care who was there. She only cared about Jesus. She was saying yes to Him and the crowd wouldn't stop her. It didn't matter how they looked at her or what they said about her. No one had ever affected her in this way. Standing behind him weeping, she let down her hair and began to use it to wipe the dirt off of Jesus's feet with her tears.

Jesus's feet would have been filthy after walking around in the dust all day. Her tears turned the dust to mud and she wiped it with her long, beautiful hair. Once His feet were clean she poured perfume over them and began to kiss them. The sinful woman invited Jesus all the way in that afternoon. She didn't hesitate in her response to His presence.

I am tempted to say we cannot respond appropriately to Jesus and care what other people think. If I won a million dollars, I would tell everyone. I would talk about it all the time and not worry if other people were annoyed. It would be a big deal, because it would completely change my life and the life of my family. I would pay off my house, buy a new car, take my family on a dream vacation, and find a lot of other really great things to do.

I have a Savior who has completely changed my life and given me more satisfaction than a million dollars could ever give and yet my response is shamefully less than. Even though I did not deserve it, He died for me. He took my broken, messed-up life and made it whole again. He gave me hope and a future. He restored me and made me new. He makes time to meet with me, gives me hope when I need it, encouragement when I am down, and strength when I am weak. He is everything to me and yet I sometimes forget to respond to Him appropriately. I sometimes worry about who else is in the room and who my response might offend.

Where do you need faith to respond? Where is God showing up in your life waiting for you to acknowledge Him? It starts with just one step. With one step you will gain the confidence necessary to take the next step. We don't have to be confident in our ability to move mountains. We don't even have to recognize the mountain. He sees it. He is fully aware of what it will take to get to the other side. He will move it. Our confidence comes in His ability.

Lately, in the challenge to grow my faith, I've started asking God to tell me things for other people. I have a desire to share His dreams for the people I interact with. Every day I ask God to help me see people the way He sees them. The other night while sitting with some friends of mine, I confessed how discouraged I was that I didn't feel like God was responding.

Trying to better understand my dilemma or perhaps hoping I would recognize what was really keeping my faith from growing, my friends questioned me. "What would it look like for God to be responding to you?" they asked. I quickly responded, "It would just be nice if He would let me know I was hearing him right and then stepping out wouldn't feel so foolish." Even as I said it, I recognized how wrong I was in my thinking. Where is the faith if I already know?

That night in bed, I felt God remind me. I already had what I was looking for.

Is it possible you already have what you've been asking for? Could He be waiting on you to step out? Faith comes from hearing and it grows with doing. If you have heard, then you need to do. "We are not disqualified by our doubts. We are often distracted by our shortcomings and our sense of limitation, but the reality is, it's not about us—it's about Him." [7]

As it often happens in my life, the very next morning God gave me the opportunity to follow Him with what He said. I was at Addy's soccer game. It was cold, wet, and way too early in the morning. As if all that weren't enough, my friend Michelle, the head coach, was out of town and I was filling in for her. Put me on a field with teenagers and I will play all day long, but early-morning soccer with whiny five-year-olds, helicopter parents and wet grass is not my idea of a good time.

Kaylee was the youngest on the team. She was afraid of soccer. The ball scared her. The goal scared her. The whistle scared her. She wouldn't even come out of the car if the referee was a boy. It had been a long season for little Kaylee. She spent more time running off the field crying than she did playing soccer. Regardless of her struggle, her mom and dad were consistent. They stuck it out. I was proud of them, they were at every game, every practice, cheering her on, not letting her quit, pushing aside the fear of judgment from other parents and trusting it was all going to come together.

This Saturday, something was different. Kaylee showed up to play! Within the first five minutes, she scored two goals. I wouldn't have believed it, had I not been standing on the field myself. She kicked the ball more times in those first six minutes then she had all season! The look on her mom's face was priceless. Her hard work and dedication paid off. Every bribe, every struggle, every fit, they were all worth these few moments of soccer-mom glory.

I watched as she celebrated her daughter and I felt like God gave me insight into her world. He was so proud of her and He wanted her to know he valued her tenacity. He delighted in her fight, in the way she stuck things out and He didn't want her to give up on the struggles she was facing outside of that soccer field either. If she would push through, she would receive the breakthrough she was looking for.

Here's where it gets hard. Let's go tell someone we don't know what God thinks about them. I didn't even know if she believed in God, let alone if she cared what He thought about her. But I was asking God for this and if I asked for revelation and never did anything with it, it would eventually stop.

Obedience to God was more important to me than the possibility of rejection I could experience through stepping out. I mustered up the courage to share with her what I felt like God was saying; she gladly received it and even allowed me to pray for her in the middle of the soccer field. Again, my faith in God grew. My confidence wasn't dependent on how she responded. My confidence grew the minute I opened my mouth. It would have grown either way. Because our confidence grows with the yes.

"Faith is the confidence that what we hope for will actually happen; it gives us assurance about things we cannot see" (Heb. 11:1 NLT).

What if it starts with just one yes? What if one yes is what gives you the confidence for the next yes? What if those two yesses are what give you the confidence necessary for the next two yesses? As you put your faith into practice, your ability to use it correctly and your confidence to trust it grow. There is a *bigger* faith available for those of us who answer. A *bigger* faith exists and will enable us to bring the Kingdom to earth in a more powerful way. We cannot bury what faith we have in the ground and expect it to grow.

Your faith can be *bigger*. It was created to be *bigger*. It's all part of the plan. Nehemiah walked the process from brokenness to *bigger* and as a result his faith grew dramatically. I just so happen to believe the same destiny waits for both of us.

chapter sixteen

Bigger in My Fight

While outlining this book, I titled this chapter "Bigger in My Fears." I thought allowing God to be *bigger* in my fears would enable me to step forward into the future I sensed Him calling me to. However, the further along in the process I journeyed, the more I realized God doesn't necessarily want to be *bigger* in our fears, He wants to be *bigger than* our fears. He wants to be *bigger* than the things threatening to derail me. *Bigger* than my worries, anxieties, and doubts. In fact, I think *bigger* changes the way we approach fear altogether. We can live with fear, we can coddle it and succumb to it, allowing it to weave its way in and out of the different areas of our lives, or we can stand up and fight it like the enemy it is.

EYE CONTACT AND RISKY STEPS

After a full day of ministry Jesus sent his tired disciples ahead of Him on the boat. He planned to dismiss the crowd, and then sneak away to spend time alone with His Father. Matthew 14 says, "Shortly before dawn Jesus went out to them, walking on the lake" (Matt. 14:25).

What interests me most in this passage is the dialogue between Jesus and Peter. Peter sees a figure in the distance, on the waves. He strains to recognize his faithful leader. As Jesus steps closer Peter remembers the events from earlier that night. He remembered the few loaves and fish and the thousands of hungry people. He remembered never running out of food. The baskets were always full! They even had leftovers! Peter didn't doubt what Jesus could do. "Jesus," he yells, "if it's really you, then tell me to come to you."

"Come," Jesus says back to His faithful follower. With one word from Jesus, Peter courageously steps out of the boat onto the dark, tossing waves and begins creeping forward.

I'm convinced one of the most hard-core things you can do with your life is make eye contact with Jesus. Locking eyes with Jesus is dangerous because He will call you out. He will invite you to join Him on His mission to bring healing and hope to everyone.

Locking eyes with Him is powerful. It's like a magnet, pulling us closer and closer. The longer we look at him, the more we believe. With each step faith grows, but also with each step, danger grows. Danger grows because as we step out, the world around us continues. Peter stepped out onto the waves because he made eye contact with Jesus. Looking into the eyes of his Master, he knew he could do anything. The waves didn't stop. The current didn't die down, simply because his bare feet were making their way to Jesus. Hesitantly Peter put one foot in front of the other. With his arms out, he steadied himself. The water was cold against his feet.

He was doing it; he was actually walking on the water! Jesus was *bigger* to him in that moment, than He had ever been before. Maybe it was the excitement, maybe it was the temperature of the water, the wind blowing around him. Whatever it was, Peter took his eyes off Jesus. With his eyes off of Jesus, he looked around. He noticed his surroundings.

Maybe Peter noticed how dark the water was or how violently it was beating against the old wooden boat. Maybe it was the intensity of the boat as it rocked back and forth or the fearful screams of the men he left behind. Whatever the reason, all of a sudden the distance between Peter and Jesus seemed to be growing instead of shrinking. As Peter noticed the wind, the waves, the darkness of the sea, he started to panic. What was he thinking? He couldn't walk on water! Why couldn't he have been patient on the ship deck with the others? Why couldn't he have simply let Jesus come all the way? In Peter's panic, he began to sink. As the ice-cold water reached his knees, he shouted out to His Master and Jesus, his ever-faithful rescuer, pulled him up.

Crippling doubt never overwhelms me when I look at Him; it overwhelms me when I stop looking at Him. When I take my eyes off Jesus and focus on the circumstances surrounding me, my doubt threatens to sink me.

Peter saw Jesus approaching on the water and called out to Him, "Is it really you, Lord?" I can't tell you how many times that exact statement has come out of my mouth. "Is that really you, Lord, asking me to speak? Is that really you, Lord, giving me that thought? Is that really you, Lord, wanting me to reach out?" Sometimes in the excitement of recognizing His voice, I step out onto the waves without noticing. As quickly as I've stepped, I realize what I have done and fear sweeps in to take over. Fear is sneaky like that. It will get you when you aren't looking. It will redirect your eyes to the distorted objects lurking in the dark corners. As the waves threaten to overturn us and fear takes over, the voice of Jesus grows faint in the background. Suddenly we hear the waves, we hear the boat being tossed back and forth and the cries of those we travel with. Everything is louder when we look away.

WINNERS

Fear paralyzes because it keeps us focused on ourselves. Fight launches us forward, because it keeps us focused on Him. As an athlete there were games you knew you were going to win. Stepping onto the field for such games changed the entire experience. As a predetermined winner, you carry a different authority. There is a pep in your step and a readiness in your voice. Throughout the game, you don't feel the need to rush; instead you are patient, slowing the ball down, and making wise choices. Your confidence helps you keep the ball steady and move it down the field.

Winners read the field differently; they keep their heads up, noticing every play. They maneuver in and out of the opponent with ease. They play the game, instead of allowing the game to play them.

"Then the Spirit of the Lord came on Jahaziel son of Zechariah, the son of Benaiah, the son of Jeiel, the son of Mattaniah, a Levite and descendant of Asaph, as he stood in the assembly. He said: 'Listen, King Jehoshaphat and all who live in Judah and Jerusalem! This is what the LORD says to you: "Do not be afraid or discouraged because of this vast army. For the battle is not yours, but God's"'" (2 Chron. 20:14–15).

How different the battle looks when we remember whose battle we are fighting. How differently I approach my day when I approach as a competitor who has already won. Recognizing He has already won the battle for me changes the way I step into this world. There is a battle ahead, that's for sure. It's not always going to be easy. There will be days I want to throw in the towel, but if I will keep moving, victory is already mine.

In the place of *bigger* we begin to recognize who we are. We begin to see more clearly the presence living inside of us. I am not who I thought I was. I am a person of presence. I carry inside of me the Spirit of the living God. His Spirit lives within me, enabling me to proclaim the good news, bind up the brokenhearted, set the captives free, release the prisoners from darkness, and proclaim this is the year of the Lord's favor (Isa. 61:1-2).

He has not put in me a Spirit of fear or timidity, instead He has placed in me a Spirit of power, love, and self-discipline (2 Timothy 1:7.) Realizing whose presence and authority I carry changes the way I interact with the world. I am no longer interested in considering my surroundings. I want to focus on the One who stands before me and walk forward onto the dark waves threatening to overturn me.

God's presence has always been with His people. In the Old Testament the Israelites didn't go anywhere without the presence of God. While Moses was on Mount Sinai, he was given the instructions to build the Ark of the Covenant and the Tabernacle in which it would rest. With the Ark in front of them, they knew God was also in front of them. Each time the Israelites stopped to camp, the Tent of Meeting would be set up and the presence of God would rest upon it.

> Then the cloud covered the tent of meeting, and the glory of the LORD filled the tabernacle. Moses could not enter the tent of meeting because the cloud had settled on it and the glory of the LORD filled the tabernacle. In all the travels of the Israelites, whenever the cloud lifted from above the tabernacle, they would set out; but if the cloud did not lift, they did not set out—until the day it lifted. So the cloud of the LORD was over the tabernacle by day, and fire

was in the cloud by night, in the sight of all the Israelites during all their travels"(Exod. 40:34-38).

Every day and every night the Lord made Himself known to His people. They weren't traveling alone. He was with them. He went before them, showing them the way to the Promised Land.

Fast forward to the New Testament and in John 1:14 it says, "The Word became flesh and tabernacled among us." John was talking about Jesus. God's desire to be with His people led Him to send His Son. The Israelites traveled with the Tabernacle. Everywhere they went, the tabernacle went. They always had God's presence in front of them. Jesus became human and tabernacled with the people. He walked with His people. Wherever Jesus was, the presence of God was, because Jesus was the carrier of the presence.

No wonder crowds flocked to Him. No wonder the sick cried out for Him. Jesus was the presence of God in the flesh. Having Jesus in the room changes everything. Imagine the way we interact when we walk into every room with Jesus by our side. Imagine the way our conversations change. Imagine the hope we bring into every hopeless situation. By themselves, the disciples were unschooled, ordinary men. With Jesus, they were unstoppable.

As Jesus prepared to leave His disciples, He prepared them to receive His Spirit. They would no longer have to be with Jesus to bring the Kingdom of heaven to earth, His presence would soon tabernacle inside of them. They would be carriers of the presence. Jesus said, "I will ask the Father, and he will give you another advocate to help you and be with you forever— the

Spirit of truth" (John 14:16–17). Jesus would soon be gone, but their access to heaven would be stronger than ever.

DESIRING HIS PRESENCE

If the Spirit of God living inside of you today were gone tomorrow would you notice the difference? Three years ago, I discovered Dave's grandma makes the best no-bake cookies in the world. They are amazing! I only wish I had tried them when we first got married—I had no idea what I was missing. The biggest argument in the Dooley house through the holidays has now become who ate the most no-bake cookies.

I eat them quickly. Dave savors them. He can make one box last three entire months. I am lucky if they last three days. I want to have control, but the presence of the no-bake cookie is too much for me to handle. They call me out of bed in the middle of the night. They distract me from the laundry in the middle of the day. They convince me to run one more mile on the treadmill, so I can justify savoring one more cookie. I am consumed with the presence of the no-bake cookie.

To avoid the tension this year we tried a different approach. Upon receiving our cookies, I separated them into two boxes. Handing Dave his box, I said, "Hide these, don't let me see where, don't put them somewhere I may accidently stumble upon them and don't ever get them out in front of the girls, because they will show me. These are your cookies and I am not guaranteeing my ability to walk away from them should I find them." Dave hid his box. I never did find them. It's quite possible they are still somewhere in our house. I, however, succumbed to the temptation and spent the next forty-eight hours eating no-bake cookies. I had them for breakfast. I had them for lunch. I had them for dinner and yes, I even had them in the middle of the night. My reasoning: the quicker I ate them the quicker they would be gone!

You might be laughing, but you know where I'm going. When is the last time you have desired God so much that it consumed your thoughts and changed the focus of your day? When is the last time we changed our direction simply because He spoke? When is the last time we stopped dead in our tracks and read-justed our schedules because He was moving somewhere else?

I want His voice to beckon me out of bed in the middle of the night. I want His voice to change my focus, change my direction, and change my schedule. I want to hear Him over all the other noise in my life. Coming into the presence of God is life chang-ing and will leave you completely transformed, but learning to live as a person of presence is revolutionary. The Holy Spirit inside of us doesn't fear, He fights because He is confident of the winner.

Moses desired God's presence above all else. He met with God and talked to him like one friend does to another. God called Moses to Mount Sinai to present the law for His people. During Moses's time away the Israelites grew impatient. They longed for a leader. Taking matters into their own hands, they emptied all their gold into the fire and made idol gods to worship. God was angry at the state of His people; He was hurt to think they could so easily be led astray. He would follow through with His promise of taking them to the Promised Land, but He was not going with them. He was done with them looking at everything but Him.

Moses and the Israelites spent years wandering through the desert searching for the Promised Land. They were all ready to be finished with this treacherous journey, but the thought of going without the presence of God terrified Moses. He pleaded with God, "If your Presence does not go with us, do not send us up from here" (Exod. 33:15). Moses was not interested in the promises of God without the presence of God. Moses understood what the Israelites didn't: God's promises are good, but they could never compare to His presence.

God was pleased with Moses's desire for Him and because of that He agreed to stay with His people. For most of us, the conversation with God would have ended right there, but not for Moses. He should be happy, right? He had just convinced God to go with them, but even that was not enough, Moses wanted more, "Then Moses said, 'Now show me your glory'" (Ex. 33:18). Moses so desires the presence of God, he asks for even more. He was eaten up with it. God's presence called out to him wherever he went, it drew him in wherever he was. He couldn't get enough of it.

STEP ONTO THE FIELD

"Do not be conformed to this present world, but be transformed by the renewing of your mind" (Rom. 12:2 NET).

I used to think this verse was about the way I saw the world. If I allowed God to transform my mind, I would look at sin differently. With a transformed mind, I wouldn't desire to be a part of anything threatening to take me away from God's best. Even though I still think this is truth, I am learning a transformed mind is much more than simply changing the way I look at the world. A transformed mind changes the way I look at myself. With a transformed mind, I see myself the way God sees me. With a transformed mind, I recognize who lives inside of me. With a transformed mind, my focus shifts from fear to fight.

That night on the water, Peter's mind was conformed. Instead of keeping his eyes locked on Jesus and recognizing whose presence he was in, he recognized the power of the waves and gave in to fear. Had he only focused on the presence, things would have been different. The more I focus on the presence of God inside of me, the more I am able to overcome, because the more focused I am on Him, the less focused I am on them.

Where are your eyes? Whose presence are you carrying? What authority are you facing your overwhelming fears with? You get to step onto the field victorious, knowing the battle has already been won. Nothing you are facing is impossible for the Spirit tabernacling inside of you.

MOVE WITH EASE

As I'm typing this I am on a plane returning to the United States. I just spent the past ten days with some amazing people serving orphans in Jos, Nigeria. It was life-changing. My pictures will never do it justice. God's voice was so loud. His promptings were so clear. The level of brokenness so intense. The need for *bigger*, so in your face. I've never sweat so much! I can't wait to take a real shower, drink coffee with real creamer, and not go to bed under a mosquito net.

The trip was dangerous, but I was surprised at the way we moved through each day with ease. There weren't many moments when

I felt fearful of my surroundings. The scariest leg of the journey was traveling the long, dirt, country road connecting Jos to Abuja.

After eight amazing days in Jos, I was sad to leave, but greatly anticipating rejoining my family back in the United States. The majority of our team crammed into the nicely air-conditioned rental van while Dave, my friend Renee, and I opted for the non-air-conditioned, less-crowded option. On people overload, I gladly gave up the air conditioning at the thought of having an entire van to myself for the five-hour drive.

Had someone told us ahead of time that not having air conditioning would be the least of our problems, maybe we would have reconsidered, but there we were, traveling way too fast, on barely paved, dusty roads, surrounded by an environment forcing us more and more outside our comfort zone.

The road is littered with army checkpoints. At each checkpoint, Nigerian soldiers carrying automatic weapons waited to greet us. It was extremely intimidating and something I could live the rest of my life not having to do again. Small tribal villages usually line the sides of each checkpoint. At each village the people would greet us with opportunities to purchase merchandise of all types. In one stop I could buy gum, windshield wipers, dead chickens, and a baby present for the shower I had coming up. I've never seen anything like it.

Thirty minutes into the drive, I noticed a commotion going on in the front of the van. Dave and Alfonzo, our Nigerian driver, seemed to be struggling to keep the van from overheating. In order to conserve the engine, Alfonzo would turn off the van and coast downhill every opportunity he had. When that tactic stopped working, Dave turned the heat on full blast to cool things down under the hood. That too, proved to only work for a little while. Maybe losing the ability to shift gears had to do with the overheating engine, maybe it didn't. Either way, next the gearshift went out.

I sat in the middle row of the fifteen-passenger van and prayed over and over again. I prayed for God to get us to Abuja. I prayed for God to give us a new engine. I prayed for the old engine to start working. As the engine continued to die and my husband continued to make the necessary adjustments to keep us going, I prayed for anything I could think of.

I don't do cars (I barely pump my own gas). I know nothing about them or how to take care of them. But my husband does. He loves cars and can fix anything! I am so thankful Dave and Alfonso were speaking some car language I didn't understand that afternoon. My cluelessness left me out of the loop and less panicked than I would have been inside the loop. Only being able to pick up some of the details being discussed in the front seat left me much more equipped to keep my eyes on Jesus instead of the waves threatening to overtake us (or in this case the sea of scary, armed military soldiers).

All of the sudden I heard a loud pop and the van jerked to the left. Because God knew I needed to finish this chapter on the plane ride home, we ran over a nail and popped our back tire. Alfonso steered the van to the side of the road and jumped out to survey the damage. I watched in disbelief as our partner van in front of us grew smaller and smaller, seemingly unaware we were falling behind. My heart sank deep into my stomach. I may have struggled to understand what was going on with the gearshift and the overheating engine, but I knew what a blown tire meant. Looking around at the miles and miles of dirt hills and mountains, I thought to myself, *This is how people die in third world countries. They get a flat tire on the side of a dangerous road with thousands of dollars worth of luggage packed away in back and no one to call for help.*

I'm not sure I have ever seen Dave move so quickly. Without a word, both he and Alfonzo jumped out of the van and got to work. The jack to hoist the van up looked like it wouldn't hold up a bike, but somehow it lifted the van, luggage and all. Our popularity grew as more and more of our non-English-speaking, Nigerian village people made their way over to check out the scene.

I'm laughing now as I imagine what they must have been thinking. Each car that drove by slowed down to peer into the van. With Dave and Alfonso under the back tire on the opposite side I'm sure they wondered what Renee and I were doing sitting, stranded, helpless on the side of the road. Every once in a while someone would walk by, stick their head in the van, look at the luggage, look at us and then say something in a language I didn't understand and keep moving.

I remember thinking, "These are the scenes that make it into the movies," but in my heart I kept praying, "Okay Jesus, you prepare the road before me. This is not outside of your hands." The danger before us was real. It wasn't in our heads, but as we pressed into the Spirit of God living inside of us the fear seemed to subside and be replaced with peace.

My husband is my hero and I'm convinced he could outwork any pit-crew team member in the country. When we needed him the most, he stepped up and hit it out of the park. He didn't focus on the waves threatening to take us over. He kept his eyes in front of him, didn't panic, and did what he knew to do. With the spare tire in place, we slammed the doors and jumped back onto the road.

From that point on I truly believe the three of us prayed that van into Abuja. Each time the heat threatened to take us down, I prayed. Each time the gears refused to shift, I prayed. Each time we stalled in the middle of an intersection because we were forced to downshift, I prayed. Panic was not an option. Fear was not a choice.

Danger is external. Fear is internal. To some extent, we don't necessarily choose the external circumstances we find ourselves in. We do, however, choose how we respond to them. At any given moment, I can allow the danger around me to take over my mind and turn to fear. When I take my trust out of the hands of my Savior and try to hold my future myself, fear and panic always seem to follow close behind. I don't remember panicking on that road headed toward Abuja, because we didn't. Fear didn't grip us, peace did. His presence was tangible and His presence brought comfort.

When Peter noticed what was around him, he panicked. In his panic he forgot who he was.

SLOW AND STEADY

"Even though I walk through the darkest valley, I will fear no evil, for you are with me; your rod and your staff, they comfort me" (Ps. 23:4).

As a shepherd, David would have known what it was like to walk through a dark valley. Any time a shepherd moved his sheep from one location to the next they would often have to travel through the valleys. In the open valleys their sheep were prey for the hungry vultures circling above. As the shepherd led his sheep his eyes were always moving and his ears always listening. Upon hearing something, the shepherd would slow down, turn his long staff around and use the hook to pull his sheep back to safety.

Slowing down to recognize who walks with me changes the way I walk. Even when things are hard, even if there is no end in sight, even if it seems all is lost. One thing is certain, He is beside you. He will never leave you. He will never forsake you. When we rely more on the circumstances surrounding us than we do on the Holy Spirit living within us, fear is the by-product.

As my desire to be a person of presence increases, my fear of what this world can do to me decreases. When the presence of God takes over our minds and our hearts, we march forward with a new confidence. Fear is no match for God tabernacling inside of you. Do you realize who you are? The power you carry? The authority you walk in? You are a person of presence. Every place you set foot you are stepping on ground He has already won for you. You do not walk alone. Fear changes to fight when we recognize who we are.

LEAVE IT ALL ON THE FIELD

My high school soccer coach used to tell us during many of his famous half-time speeches, "Leave it all on the field." In other words, if you are going to fight, then fight. Give it all you've got. Don't walk away from a battle and wonder if you could have given more. Don't fear having your heart broken. Push to the point of exhaustion. Know you gave everything you possibly could and then trust God to do the rest.

"In all these things we are more than conquerors through him who loved us. For I am convinced that neither death nor life, neither angels nor demons, neither the present nor the future, nor any powers, neither height nor depth, nor anything else in all creation, will be able to separate us from the love of God that is in Christ Jesus our Lord" (Rom. 8:37–39).

We all have something to conquer. Conquerors don't fear, they fight. The outcome has already been determined. Nothing can separate you from the presence you carry within you. Nothing can overcome what He already overcame. He defeated death, He overcame sin, He was victorious and He lives in us. We get to claim His presence and with His presence we celebrate in His victory. Carry His presence boldly, step onto the field courageously, and fight for the *bigger*.

chapter seventeen

Bigger in My Future

The natural by-product of allowing God to be *bigger* in all of your life is, He will also become *bigger* in your future. Approaching the future as though we are in control is limiting. In control, we go after things within reach instead of those right outside of our grasp. God is not interested in what we can do for Him; He is interested in what we can do with Him. A *bigger* future involves the ability to hold tight to Jesus and loosely to everything else.

I love how the Bible refers to Joseph as a dreamer. Somewhere deep inside all of us lives a dreamer, a lot like Joseph. God gave Joseph a dream. One day his brothers would bow down to him. One day the sun and the stars would obey him. One day he would rule the nation. At such a young age, this powerful dream seemed unclear. Joseph struggled, trying to figure out where his first move should be. What was his role in the future? Was this dream his responsibility to carry out?

Joseph quickly took ownership of the dream God gave him. He was young and too immature to know that only God controls the *bigger*. God saw what Joseph wasn't capable of seeing. God saw the process. He recognized who Joseph was, but more importantly He recognized who Joseph would become.

At seventeen, Joseph was not yet who he needed to be in order to handle such a lofty dream. God had to do a work in him, before He could shoulder the responsibility of the work He intended to do through Him.

At the onset of the dream, Joseph rushed out to share with his older brothers the future vision God let him in on.

"We were binding sheaves of grain out in the field when suddenly my sheaf rose and stood upright, while your sheaves gathered around mine and bowed down to it" (Gen. 37:7).

It helps if you fully understand the history there. Joseph's brothers already didn't like him. Joseph was the youngest and by far his father's favorite son. As a symbol of his affection Joseph's father gave him a robe to wear. It was long and colorful, something typically reserved for royalty. Even though Joseph was the youngest, his father esteemed him high above his brothers. As you could imagine, Joseph's brothers were none too thrilled at the thought of bowing down to their cocky little brother.

Shortly after the dream conversation took place, Joseph's father sent him to check on his brothers, as they worked in the field. The brothers, still reeling from Joseph's offensive dream, saw him approaching and began to talk of the things they'd like to do to him. Their annoyance quickly turned to anger and before they knew it they were plotting to kill their little brother. "Here comes that dreamer!" they said to each other. "Come now, let's kill him and throw him into one of these cisterns and say that a ferocious animal devoured him. Then we'll see what comes of his dreams" (Gen. 37:19–20).

Thankfully, there was Reuben. Reuben, the oldest brother, tried to rescue Joseph from their hands. "'Let's not take his life,' he said. 'Don't shed any blood. Throw him into this cistern here in the wilderness, but don't lay a hand on him'" (Gen. 37:21–22).

When Joseph reached his brothers, they stripped him of his robe and threw him into a nearby cistern. Then they sat down to eat their meal, as though nothing happened. While they were eating, a caravan of Ishmaelites passed by. Deciding perhaps they should profit off of their little brother, they sold him to the Ishmaelites as a slave.

Once in Egypt, Jacob was sold to Potiphar, who worked for the king. Joseph, the dreamer, had now become Joseph, the slave. The Bible says the Lord was with Joseph, even as a slave. Joseph had favor on Potiphar's estate and was quickly put in charge of the entire household. Joseph also found favor with Potiphar's wife. She pursued him over and over, trying to get him to come to bed with her. But Joseph refused her.

Many times over Joseph denied Potiphar's wife, until one afternoon she would not take no for an answer. She threw herself at Joseph, demanding he go to bed with her. Joseph, recognizing the trouble he was in, took off running. In the rage of rejection, Potiphar's wife took hold of Joseph's shirt and literally ripped it off his body. Feeling scorned, she took the shirt and used it as evidence against Joseph. If she couldn't have him, no one would. She accused Joseph of raping her, leaving Potiphar no choice but to put him in prison.

No doubt, as Joseph sat in prison, he struggled. Joseph, the dreamer, had become Joseph, the slave, and now he was Joseph, the prisoner. What he may not have realized was, even while he was behind bars God was working. Joseph gained favor with the prison warden and the warden quickly put him in charge of the daily operations. The warden trusted Joseph so much he paid no attention to anything under Joseph's care.

"Some time later, the cupbearer and the baker of the king of Egypt offended their master, the king of Egypt. Pharaoh was angry with his two officials, the chief cupbearer and the chief baker, and put them in custody in the house of the captain of the guard, in the same prison where Joseph was confined. The captain of the guard assigned them to Joseph, and he attended them. After they had been in custody for some time, each of the two men—the cupbearer and the baker of the king of Egypt, who were being held in prison—had a dream the same night, and each dream had a meaning of its own" (Gen. 40:1–5).

It was clear the cupbearer and baker were struggling with something. They confessed to Joseph the disturbing dreams both had experienced. The lack of answers left them confused. After listening to their dreams Joseph replied, "Do not interpretations belong to God? Tell me your dreams" (Gen. 40:8).

This statement shows a subtle turning point in Joseph's life. Here we get a glimpse of how Joseph is maturing in his faith. Years earlier, when he had a dream, he was quick to interpret the meaning, and even quicker to start the work of making it happen. But Joseph's response this time shows he was beginning to see how the process works. Dreams, or interpretations of dreams, were not his to own. It was God who gave dreams and it would be God who interpreted them. Maybe young Joseph was beginning to see the journey was a marathon and not a sprint.

The seventeen-year-old dreamer he used to be was not yet the person he needed to be to walk out such a weighty dream. Joseph was surrendered to the process of becoming the person God needed him to be to own the dream he had been given years ago.

Both prisoners told Joseph their dreams and Joseph, with God's help, interpreted them honestly. Upon the release of the cupbearer and baker, Joseph asked Pharaoh's men to remember him. Because God is good at bring dreams to fruition, the cupbearer's and baker's dreams played out just as Joseph predicted. Unfortunately, Pharaoh's men forgot about Joseph.

Being overlooked is no fun, especially when you have a dream, but here was Joseph, disregarded again. How did he get to this place in life? How could he have had such dreams only to wind up in the middle of nowhere? Had he been wrong all along? Those first few days he was so sure and look at him now; betrayed by his own brothers, sold into slavery, falsely accused, flung into prison and forgotten. No one would blame him for giving up and replacing his dreams with something more attainable.

FORGOTTEN DREAMS

I have replaced dreams with more attainable dreams. I have lost hope in things that seemed too far off. Even things I thought God had shown me. I have written off the desires of my heart, to avoid the pain of being overlooked. It's always easier to settle into the tangible. It's always easier to grab for what you can reach.

Bigger is not something we can usher in by ourselves. On this side of the dream the tallest challenge can sometimes be mustering up the courage to keep believing.

Joseph was overlooked for two full years until Pharaoh himself had a dream no one could interpret. It was only then that the cupbearer remembered Joseph. He told Pharaoh, "'Today I am reminded of my shortcomings Pharaoh was once angry with his servants, and he imprisoned me and the chief baker in the house of the captain of the guard. Each of us had a dream the same night, and each dream had a meaning of its own. Now a young Hebrew was there with us, a servant of the captain of the guard.

We told him our dreams, and he interpreted them for us, giving each man the interpretation of his dream. And things turned out exactly as he interpreted them to us: I was restored to my position, and the other man was impaled" (Gen. 41:9–13).

Joseph was quickly brought out of prison, given a change of clothes and placed in front of Pharaoh. "Pharaoh said to Joseph'I had a dream, and no one can interpret it. But I have heard it said of you that when you hear a dream you can interpret it" (Gen. 41:15).

Joseph's response to Pharaoh says it all, "I cannot do it, . . . but God will" (Gen. 41:16). I cannot, but God will. He had come full circle. The interpretation was completely up to God. Joseph could do his part by listening, but then he had to rely on God to bring the rest. Joseph no longer needed any credit. He was now, more than ever, aware of God's role in carrying out his dreams.

Our dreams, whether big or small, are for God, because our dreams are from God. No matter what dreams He puts on our heart, we can be sure He has put them there to benefit the Kingdom. Joseph was given this dream because this dream would have an eternal impact on the Kingdom of God. Pursuing our dreams for any reason other than to reveal His Kingdom and bring Him glory will leave us empty-handed and right back where we started.

Our job is not to control the dreams God places in our hearts; instead, we are to hand them back to Him and trust as He works out the details. *Bigger* dreams are not something we accomplish on our own. If we could accomplish *bigger* dreams on our own, why would we need to be connected to Him in the first place?

God doesn't get glory when we do what we are capable of doing. He gets glory when we do what only He is capable of doing.

God gave Joseph what he needed to interpret Pharaoh's dream. Joseph's prediction led to more opportunities for the leadership God had been preparing him for all along. Just like that, Joseph was put in charge of all of Egypt. From dreamer, to slave, to prisoner, to commander in chief, Joseph witnessed the hand of God at work in his dream.

God is more capable than we give Him credit for. Had Joseph's dream been left to him to produce, it's no telling where he would have landed. I am certain he never envisioned that after years of slavery and prison, his brothers would come to him, leader of the free world, bow down and beg for food, exactly the way he envisioned it as a seventeen-year-old boy. Yet, here he was, leading Egypt through one of the most trying times ever. God's dreams for Joseph were *bigger* than he ever asked or imagined possible.

IN THE MIDDLE

We live in an instant world. We are spoiled by instant access, instant weight loss and instant success. If something takes any amount of time, we have been programmed to think it must not be working. Joseph, like Nehemiah, had a big dream and his first reaction was to jump in and get to work.

"God delights in small beginnings" (Zech. 4:10)

Fortunately, we serve a God who thrives in the middle. The middle is where the plot thickens. The middle is where intimacy is acquired, where love is found, where tension builds. Think about it, would you ever watch a movie if you were only able to see the first and last ten minutes of it? We would never do that. The middle is where the movie comes to life.

I think God doesn't always work in the instant, because He so loves the middle. He sees the value of the plot. He recognizes what we will learn, how we will grow, and all the changes that will take place in us as we daily surrender to him. We celebrate greatness and achievement, but God celebrates the beginning. God takes our small beginnings and uses them to lead us to His dreams and His purposes. He uses them to shape us and direct us. He uses them to grow our faith and push us forward. He uses them to teach us humility, dependence, and grace. It is in the middle that we become the people we need to be to handle the *bigger* dreams of God.

As I followed Jesus, I began to recognize a dream in my heart. Because of that dream, I agreed to teach a middle school Sunday school class. I had no idea how to teach. In all reality, I taught myself more than I taught them. While Jesus worked to rebuild my walls, I devoted my energy to learning. I was in over my head, but growing from the challenge. Sometime during those early morning classes, God planted a dream in my heart to speak and write as a means of pointing others toward transformation.

God has a dream for you. Your dream will come to life in the middle. It is shaped out of your yesses. In your yesses, you get a dream. As you follow Him, He will guide you down the right path and then out of nowhere, you will find it. In the middle of your path, you will find your dream. The small beginnings matter so much because it is in those small beginnings we are able to take the first steps toward the *bigger* dreams of God.

God used every part of Joseph's life to mold him into the person he needed to be to walk out his dream. That arrogant seventeen-year-old boy, living at home with his father and brothers, was not the same man standing before Pharaoh giving God full credit. Your dreams are never impossible with God. Take what feels out of reach and hand it back to Him.

"Whatever you do, do it all for the glory of God" (1 Cor. 10:31). I love this because it's whatever. Whatever you do, however you do it, wherever you do it. Do what you want, do what you love, do what you are good at, just be sure to do it for the glory of God. Our dreams are formed as we do what we do for His glory.

DO WHAT YOU DO

God wants you in this world, living for His name. He wants to partner with you to make His goodness known. Don't do what you do for your own glory, that's boring. *Bigger* is doing things you love for God's glory. *Bigger* is using your passion to point others to the Kingdom.

You love math, that's great, I needed people like you in my life. But don't simply be a math teacher because you love the thrill of dividing fractions. Be a math teacher because you love the opportunity to love students the way Jesus loves students. Be a math teacher because you love seeking out lonely students and encouraging them the way you believe the Father would. Don't only do what you love to do because you love to do it. Do it because God created you to do it. Do it to inspire others. Do it to speak over them. Do it to lift Him up before this world.

Joseph didn't get to have a dream because he was a rock star. Joseph was an ordinary person; his dreams were all about God. He received a dream, but he was able to keep his dream because over the course of time he learned to surrender. He surrendered his dream to the only person fully capable of doing something with it. He was able to walk out his dream because he was willing to walk the process to *bigger*. He walked it out, even as a hated brother, even as a slave, and even as a prisoner.

I talk to people about Jesus. It's what I do. Before I knew Jesus, I talked to people for my own glory. I connected with people based on what I would get out of the relationship, not what I could bring to the relationship. One of my other strengths is WOO. WOO stands for winning others over. It basically means I can talk people into just about anything, not because I manipulate them, but because I truly believe whatever it is I am doing is the best thing they could be doing. Another strength of mine is belief. Belief leads me to genuinely believe in things. Not just believe, but believe, believe. If I am doing it, then you should be doing it too, because it is obviously the best thing we could be doing. The doing it together part comes into play because my final strength is being an includer. Why do something alone when you can do it with someone else? In my world, the more people, the better. As an includer who believes her job (telling people about Jesus) is the best, and not only wants everyone to join in, but is actually gifted at making them really want to, I work to glorify God.

Using what I am good at for my glory looked different than using it for God's glory. As a teenager who didn't love Jesus, I spent my teen years talking people into being a part of ridiculous sin. This is, until Jesus got ahold of me and changed my heart. He turned me around and showed me what life was all about. He opened my eyes to a completely new world. He didn't change what I was good at. I am still the same person, with the same strengths. The only difference is now I do it all for the glory of God.

If you will give me enough time, I will talk you into it. I will tell you how crazy awesome Jesus is and how He radically changed my life. I will tell you about the plans He has for you. I will tell you of His promises and His goodness, His grace and His mercy. I will keep talking until you walk away or decide to join me, because that's who I am.

Learning how to hand my dreams back to God changed my life. Who wants to settle for a *bigger* you can accomplish yourself when you can run after a *bigger* only He can achieve?

IN THE END

Yosselin got a new house because a team of people came together to do what they were already naturally good at. God planted a dream in my heart that cold January afternoon as we sat in their driveway crying over what seemed to be impossible. He planted a dream in my heart to build this little girl and her family a new house. At that place, on that day, I was so weak I couldn't even see this dream was from Him, for me.

But over the course of the next eleven months, as we continually gave our dream back to God, He empowered us to walk forward. He provided us the resources and people necessary to continue step by step, day by day. It wasn't about me. It wasn't only my dream. It was God's dream He shared with me. As long as I did what I was good at with Him in mind, God would work it out. I spent eleven months telling people how big God was and talking them into letting us spend their money or use their time and talents for His glory.

Maybe you don't think you have a dream. Maybe you had a dream, but wrote it off long ago and think it is too late. Maybe you thought you had your dream only to have it ripped from your hands. Maybe your dream has been shattered into a million pieces. Maybe you jumped the gun, like Joseph, and tried to get the dream accomplished on your own. Whatever it is, whatever has happened, whatever hasn't happened, I want you to know, I believe He has something for you. You may not recognize it; I didn't recognize it at first either. Even after identifying it, I was unable to speak it out loud for years because of fear.

What if He is waiting for you to speak it out loud? What if speaking it out loud is God's way of helping you recognize who is in control? What if saying it out loud is your first step in letting go—letting go of fear, letting go of control, letting go of doubt, regret, anger, anxiety?

If I were sitting there with you I would ask you to tell me your dream, because I recognize the power in saying it out loud. I recognize the power in not having an answer and also the power in having too many answers. Can we try it, anyway? I know I am not there and you may be in the middle of a public place (if you are, you can whisper so no one thinks you are crazy), but will you take a risk and finish this sentence for me?

I think God's dream for me might be _____

_____ .

God can handle your dream. He will be gentle with your heart. It's not going to be an easy journey, but you can trust Him.

"Do not all interpretations belong to God?" (Gen. 40:8).

Following Christ is about living a life other people benefit from. That's the fruit of who Jesus is. He would not give us a dream if it didn't benefit someone else. It would go against His character. Other people's dreams have greatly affected mine. I am writing this right now because I have people in my life who said yes to following Jesus. In their yesses they got a dream and as they walked out their dreams, God used them to impact me. Their yes impacted my yes.

God is piecing together a *bigger* story. Joseph's dream wasn't only about Joseph. God is so much *bigger* than that. Joseph's dream was about the future of Joseph's family and the future of God's people.

I am learning so much right now as I hand my dreams back to God. As I surrender my dreams to Him, He will use them to impact the people around me: my husband, my girls, my family, my closest friends, and people I don't even know. This is the reason building Yosselin a new house wasn't even about her getting a new house. It was simply the story God was writing so the world could see how big He is. It was about everyone who tuned in to the local news stations the night before Thanksgiving and received a glimpse of who God was to a hurting family in a neighborhood nearby. It was about the people who prayed healing over her body. It was about the public schools and administration having a way to bring God into daily life. I was about the men and women who still find me and continue to ask about Yosselin's cancer. It was about the people who never prayed for people before, but felt moved to pray for Yosselin. It was about new faith being built and old faith being restored.

The enemy wins when we allow shame, fear, or discouragement to keep us in a nondreaming state of living. Go after your dream because believing in *bigger* is the best thing you can do for you, but also go after your dream because your dream will impact the lives of the people around you.

I sat with a woman yesterday at a coffee shop and talked about Jesus. The Holy Spirit was doing a number on her and she was feeling the conviction that comes from living a life separated from Jesus. She was struggling to say yes to what God was calling her to because she knew her husband wasn't ready yet. The truth is, the best thing she can do for her husband is say yes to Jesus. Her yes will have an affect on his yes. When God goes to work on her life and begins to shape her and grow her, His glory will be made known through her. As she gets a dream and hands her dream back to God, the people closest to her will be impacted. Her dreams will inspire them, challenge them and call them to respond.

A small God would give us dreams just for us, but a big God gives us dreams with the potential to shape hundreds, even thousands. A small God would give us attainable dreams, but a big God gives us scary, out-of-reach dreams, forcing us to depend on Him in ways we never imagined. A small God gives temporary rewards, which feel great in the instant, but fade over our lifetime. A big God gives rewards that last for all eternity.

"'I know the plans I have for you,' declares the LORD, 'plans to prosper you and not to harm you, plans to give you a hope and a future'" (Jer. 29:11).

He does have a plan for you. He does have a purpose for you. He created you and gifted you to be exactly who you are for a specific reason. There is no one else just like you. No one can love Him the way you love Him and serve Him the way you serve Him. There are things on this earth that will not get done if you do not start walking out the dreams He has given you. It is inevitable, you will experience heartbreak, but *bigger* is having the ability to look at heartbreak from a different perspective. Brokenness leads to *bigger*. Brokenness always leads to *bigger* when placed in the hands of the ultimate rebuilder.

YOSSELIN'S DREAM

God gave us a dream. Trying to figure it out on our own led us to remodeling a bedroom. The small step of remodeling was significant, because it was in that remodel we realized God was *bigger* than we gave Him credit for. Upon that realization we took our God-sized dream and handed it back to Him. If this was something God wanted to do, then it was His to do. We agreed to say yes and with every yes He showed up and showed off. God intended to use our dream to blow our minds.

Nehemiah had a dream. He wanted to rebuild the wall for his people. This wasn't a dream he asked for, but brokenness changed his direction and pointed him toward *bigger*. As his perspective shifted he was able to leave behind his job and join God on the journey toward *bigger*. It wasn't easy, it was terrifying, but he stuck with it. He pushed through the difficult days, fighting desperately to stay on his ladder as he climbed to *bigger*. Upon completing the wall I don't believe he looked at the future with the regret of what it cost him to get there. God had been faithful to do exactly what He promised and it really was *bigger*.

It was and always is all about God. He is writing the story. He is making His name known to the world. He is *bigger*. You are who you are because God created you to be that way. He gifted you. He gave you your passions; He gave you your visions. Dare to start dreaming about what He might do with them as you hand them back to Him. Dare to say yes to Him in a life-impacting way. Dare to dream dreams *bigger* than you ever asked or imagined possible because we most definitely serve a God who is *bigger* than we ever asked or imagined possible.

NOTES

1. Brennen Manning, *The Rabbi's Heartbeat* (Colorado Springs: NavPress, 2003), 13.

2. Mark Batterson, *The Circle Maker* (Grand Rapids: Zondervan, 2011).

3. Bill Johnson, *Face to Face with God* (Lake Mary, FL: Charisma House, 2007), 46.

4. Steven Furtick, *Sun Stand Still* (Colorado Springs: Multnomah Books, 2010), 184.

5. Oswald Chambers, *My Utmost for His Highest* (Uhrichsville, OH: Barbour, 1992), 72.

6. Robby Dawkins, *Do What Jesus Did* (Bloomington, MN: Chosen Books, 2013), 27.

7. Ibid., 32.

CPSIA information can be obtained at www.ICGtesting.com
Printed in the USA
BVOW03s1902210415

397115BV00002B/6/P